THE MODERN MILITARY AND THE ENVIRONMENT

The Laws of Peace and War

William A. Wilcox, Jr.

Government Institutes

An imprint of
THE SCARECROW PRESS, INC.
Lanham, Maryland • Toronto • Plymouth, UK
2007

Government Institutes

Published in the United States of America
by Government Institutes, an imprint of The Scarecrow Press, Inc.
A wholly owned subsidiary of
The Rowman & Littlefield Publishing Group, Inc.
4501 Forbes Boulevard, Suite 200
Lanham, Maryland 20706
http://www.govinstpress.com/

Estover Road
Plymouth PL6 7PY
United Kingdom

The reader should not rely on this publication to address specific questions that apply to a particular set of facts. The author and the publisher make no representation or warranty, express or implied, as to the completeness, correctness, or utility of the information in this publication. In addition, the author and the publisher assume no liability of any kind whatsoever resulting from the use of or reliance upon the contents of this book.

British Library Cataloguing in Publication Information Available

Library of Congress Cataloging-in-Publication Data

Wilcox, William A., Jr., 1961–
The modern military and the environment : the laws of peace and war / William A. Wilcox, Jr.
p. cm.
Includes bibliographical references and index.
ISBN-13: 978-0-86587-174-8 (pbk. : alk. paper)
ISBN-10: 0-86587-174-4 (pbk. : alk. paper)
1. Environmental law—United States. 2. Military law—Environmental aspects—United States. 3. Military bases—Environmental aspects—United States. 4. United States—Armed Forces—Environmental aspects. I. Title.
KF3779.M5W55 2007
344.7304'6—dc22 2006036228

∞™ The paper used in this publication meets the minimum requirements of American National Standard for Information Sciences—Permanence of Paper for Printed Library Materials, ANSI/NISO Z39.48-1992.
Manufactured in the United States of America.

Contents

Acknowledgments

I WOULD LIKE TO THANK Major Roburt Yale, member of the U.S. Army Reserve's First Legal Support Organization, for his timely assistance and feedback, which was critical in bringing this project to fruition. I would also like to thank Sheila Harvey and Donald Carr of the Washington, D.C., office of Pillsbury Winthrop Shaw Pittman LLP, and Colonel Robert Hough of the First LSO, for their patience and professional support.

Portions of chapters 2 and 3 were previously published as an article, "Special Issues in Environmental Law Involving Federal Agencies," which appeared in *The Villanova Environmental Law Journal* 14, no. 1, 2003. Portions of part II were previously published as an article, "Access to Environmental Information in the United States and the United Kingdom," which appeared in the *Loyola of Los Angeles International & Comparative Law Review* 23, March 2001, and are reprinted by permission. Portions of chapter 6 were previously published as an article in and are reprinted with permission from the *Environmental Liability, Enforcement & Penalties Reporter*, October 2005, "Environmental Enforcement: California and Other States Grapple with Land Use Covenants on Federal Property," Copyright© 2005, Argent Communications Group. Further copying requires additional written consent: P.O. Box 1425, Foresthill, CA 95631; e-mail: reprints@argentco.com.

Introduction:
The Military and the Environment

WHETHER DURING PEACETIME OR WAR, there is a constant tension between environmental and national security values. The preparation for war by U.S. forces involves the "train as we fight" doctrine. Computer simulators are helpful, but they cannot completely replicate actual field conditions that soldiers will endure and under which weapons systems will be used. Environmentalists often decry the damages the military forces are able to visit upon the environment with seeming impunity. And there is an undeniable history of environmental degradation that military development, testing, and training operations have caused. Environmentalists seeking greater accountability over the military services can point to a history of dumping, spilling, and stockpiling of harmful chemicals as well as bombing.

Meanwhile, military leaders point to restrictions of environmental law as imposing on readiness. Despite significant efforts to adjust to changing requirements, the tension between the mission and the environment still persists. Their concerns over restricted training due to "encroachment" by the civilian communities around military bases have threatened to shut down bases in heavily populated areas in favor of alternate locations in less developed areas. Community concerns and, at times, lawsuits over the noise or other impacts of military operations can potentially restrict the military's ability to conduct training in a manner that would fully prepare forces for war. Yet, the importance of both national security and environmental protection in our society today demands that the imperative needs of both functions be met.

Some of the claims on both sides are exaggerated, but there is more than a grain of truth to some of the claims as well. To fully understand the changing relationship between the American military and the environment, it is necessary to explore the impact of international law as it applies to environmental effects of combat operations abroad, to examine environmental law as it applies to the military at home, and to investigate the means available for getting environmental information from the government—not just the military departments but also environmental regulatory agencies—about the military's impacts on the environment. Since the national defense establishment's primary purpose is to fight an enemy, it is logical to also look at the military as it affects the environment in its intended setting—hostile warfare.

The object of this book is to provide an overview of the most common environmental issues that the military faces today, both at war and during peacetime. Its focus is on the legal framework in which environmental issues are addressed, leaving political and scientific discussions for those better qualified. In scope, this work is most similar to Professor Stephen Dycus's 1996 book *National Defense and the Environment*, although it provides the perspective of one who was intimately involved with most of the issues and includes recent developments that could not have been addressed in the earlier work. It provides a look at how policy translates into legal application. It provides a springboard for a more exhaustive examination of many issues, which would encompass a further examination of technical and political implications.

This book is not intended to be an exhaustive treatise on every aspect of environmental law applied to military activities; nor is it a comprehensive scientific analysis on environmental damages caused by the military. Rather, it provides an overview of some of the common environmental law issues that arise and that illuminate the tension between national defense and protection of the environment. The book is divided into three parts, with part I focusing on the most common issues with which the military, the public, and regulators contend in domestic environmental law—some of which are bizarre products of legal history and interpretation. Part II provides an overview of the laws governing access to information concerning the military's impacts on the environment, which is a key component in holding military services accountable for compliance with environmental requirements. Part III focuses on how the laws of war may govern the conduct of military forces toward the environment in combat. It provides an overview of environmental issues that arise in warfare and continue to be of concern to the international community. Coverage of these subject areas should be sufficient to provide environmental law practitioners and policy makers with an introduction to many of the legal authorities—including statutes, regulations, executive orders, and agency policy documents—necessary to understand the application of environmental law to military activities.

I

PEACETIME OPERATIONS

1

The Business of Defense

WE LIVE IN A HOSTILE WORLD. The tragic events of September 11, 2001, brought that realization crashing down on all of us. Despite the horror of war, it is necessary at times for a nation, especially a nation preeminent in the world, to engage in it. As a nation, since our inception we have devoted substantial resources to arming for, preparing for, and fighting wars both large and small. A nation born of war, military life and values are embedded within our culture. More recently, as our society has matured, an understanding and appreciation of the environment has taken a place alongside military readiness among our value system. Yet, the two—military and environmental values—are not always compatible with one another. The objectives of the U.S. military, during both peacetime and wartime, are often at odds with the natural environment.

Including the military, the federal government is one of the largest, if not the largest, industries in the United States. The scope of the federal government's activity is awesome. It is the largest landholder in the United States, with millions of acres. It conducts training and construction operations with major environmental impacts and operates thousands of industrial-style facilities with a constant waste stream. The federal government builds—or provides the funding for—prisons, highways, dams, power plants, office buildings, hospitals, laboratories, industrial shops, ammunition and hazardous material storage facilities, airplane hangars, and motor pools. The federal government is responsible for cattle grazing and hard rock mining on public lands, and logging in national forests.

Defense-related activities account for some of the largest environmental impacts by the federal government. Tanks maneuver through our forests, ships dock at our ports, jets soar through our skies, and satellites orbit our planet. During testing and training, the military drops explosive ordnance on the land and in the sea. In addition to the activities of the military services of the Department of Defense (DOD), the Department of Energy's National Nuclear Security Administration is responsible for the nation's nuclear weapons stockpile. The Coast Guard, which provides protection to the nation's ports, waterways, and coastlines, is now part of the Department of Homeland Security. The environmental effects of all components of the defense establishment are subject to some regulator oversight.

Professor Stephen Dycus noted a trend toward heightened scrutiny of the environmental effects of military activities. "Even before the end of the Cold War, our focus had begun to shift from the external threat of an 'Evil Empire' to the internal threat of a defense establishment sometimes heedless of its impacts on nature and human health," he wrote. "In particular, revelations about nearly a half-century of environmental neglect at America's military bases and nuclear weapons plants have brought an angry reaction from a public exposed, without its knowledge or consent, to serious health risks, and saddled with the financial burden of cleaning it all up."[1]

Yet, it seems as though the military services and other defense-related government agencies play by their own rules when it comes to environmental and natural resources regulation. Under the "Unitary Executive Doctrine," which prohibits agencies from suing one another without first going through a process to resolve an issue within the executive branch, it appears the U.S. Environmental Protection Agency (EPA) is limited in its ability to regulate other federal agencies despite its obvious authority to do so.[2] Under Executive Order 12,088, the Office of Management and Budget has authority to resolve conflicts between agencies regarding violations of environmental laws.[3]

State regulators and the public are often frustrated or confused by the special body of environmental law that applies to the federal government, including the military. Many of those concerned about the environment have difficulty understanding why the military and other federal government agencies are treated differently than private sector counterparts.[4] "For nearly fifty years, the U.S. military, the nation's largest polluter, has threatened human health and the environment with the ceaseless dumping and improper disposal of noxious chemicals throughout virtually every state," wrote one commentator. "Through widespread mishandling and mismanagement of radioactive waste, spent fuels, oils, solvents, paints, acids, heavy metals, and other hazardous materials, the Departments of Defense (DoD) and Energy

(DoE) have 'cast a chemical plague over our country,' creating a toxic legacy for the next several generations."[5]

Environmental practices at military facilities have even led to criminal prosecutions. In *United States v. Dee*,[6] the U.S. Court of Appeals for the Fourth Circuit upheld convictions of three Army employees, William Dee, Robert Lentz, and Carl Gepp, for violating various provisions of the Resource Conservation and Recovery Act (RCRA)[7] at Aberdeen Proving Ground, Maryland. The three men, senior employees of the Chemical Research, Development, and Engineering Center, had been convicted of violations relating to their handling of chemical warfare agents.[8] Among their defenses, the three contended that they were immune from criminal prosecution under RCRA because they were federal employees working at a federal facility. The appeals court held that there was "simply no merit to this suggestion."[9] The court held further that prosecutors were not required to show that the defendants knew that violating RCRA was a crime or that the chemicals they were handling were defined as hazardous wastes under RCRA. It was sufficient to show that Dee, Lentz, and Gepp knew that the chemicals were hazardous.[10]

Another commentator, calling for increasing the number of criminal prosecutions for environmental crimes at federal military facilities, asserted that "the U.S. military is indisputably the largest contributor to contamination at federal facilities. Decades of weapons testing have contaminated Army grounds, and nearly every Air Force base in the country is polluted with solvents used to 'wash' aircraft and machinery. Of over 17,000 potentially contaminated military sites," she continued, "100 are at the beginning of the National Priorities List, the Superfund program's inventory of the nation's worst contaminated sites. The Navy has released unknown quantities of paint and paint strippers into shipyard grounds and coastal waters."[11] That same commentator cited statistics that the military "produces more than a ton of toxic wastes *every minute*, creating a more ominous environmental threat than that of private companies."[12] She further cited statistics indicating that the military was slow in complying with environmental laws such as the Comprehensive Environmental Response, Compensation, and Liability Act (CERCLA),[13] stating that "the military has an unimpressive history of self-regulation and compliance."[14] "In light of the deterrence failure of environmental laws in the federal enclave," she concluded, "criminal prosecution of federal employees is currently the best deterrence mechanism available for ensuring environmental compliance and enforcement at federal facilities."[15]

No question, criminal prosecutions of federal employees can get the attention of the federal workforce, especially since federal employees usually have to pay for their own legal defense. Under the Department of Justice's (DOJ) regulations regarding representation of federal employees in civil, criminal, and congressional proceedings, DOJ may provide representation, or provide private counsel, for employees in such proceedings who are brought into proceedings because of actions performed within the scope of the employee's duties.[16] However, such representation is generally not available in federal criminal proceedings[17] or in state proceedings in which there is a potential of a federal prosecution based upon "some evidence of his specific participation in a crime."[18] Further, it is unlikely the Department of Justice would find commission of a crime to be within the scope of employment of any employee. DOJ must also find that a criminal defense of any employee is in the interest of the United States.[19] If, during the course of the proceedings, a federal employee is exonerated or otherwise demonstrates his or her actions were within the scope of duty, then that employee might be eligible for reimbursement of attorney's fees.[20] Yet, it is difficult to imagine federal service as an attractive career if employees must live in constant fear of prosecution for their actions, especially in light of the comparatively lower wages they earn. While *Dee* served as a wake-up call for federal managers and employees everywhere, the threat of prosecution is perhaps not the best means for accomplishing environmental compliance.

Still, defense is a messy business. And the techniques and equipment of wartime must be tirelessly trained and tested during peacetime. Training should be conducted under circumstances as realistic as possible and might in itself cause environmental damage. This entails use of live ammunition at times and training in and maintenance of vehicles, aircraft, and seagoing vessels of war. Many aspects of training and maintaining military forces can have significant environmental impacts.

In addition, unlike other industries that generate or work with hazardous materials as part of industrial processes, the military possesses materials that were manufactured for the purpose of killing. Some of those materials perform their missions with frightening efficiency. Chemical agents and munitions that were stockpiled for the nation's security during the Cold War are now excess to the nation's needs and must be destroyed. The international community, in the 1993 Chemical Weapons Convention, determined that the chemical stockpile should be destroyed by April 29, 2007.[21] Yet the destruction of those chemical agents poses still more environmental problems, with communities such as Anniston, Alabama, objecting to incineration of such materials near their homes.[22] The United States began to fall behind schedule, having destroyed only 8,220 tons, or 26 percent, of its stockpile by September 24, 2003.[23]

And chemical weapons destruction was not the only daunting issue facing the defense agencies after the Cold War. For instance, the Department of Energy's facility at Rocky Flats, Colorado, produced the trigger mechanisms for nearly every nuclear weapon built in the United States from 1951 to 1989, but it left behind significant amounts of radioactive wastes and contamination spurring a costly cleanup that wasn't considered completed until 2005.[24] Further, many properties contaminated by past military activities no longer belong to defense agencies. The Defense Environmental Restoration Program provides funding for environmental cleanup on both active military installations and former military properties overseen by the U.S. Army Corps of Engineers under the Formerly Used Defense Site (FUDS) program.[25]

But efforts to attain compliance with environmental laws and to clean up hazardous materials at military facilities have been undertaken during the past twenty years. The U.S. Army, for instance, which witnessed the criminal prosecutions of three of its employees in the 1980s, had made great strides during the 1990s to improve its environmental record. Adopting a "strategy into the 21st Century," the Army resolved to

1. Focus efforts on pollution prevention where and when possible to reduce or eliminate pollution at the source.
2. Conserve and preserve natural and cultural resources so they will be available for present and future generations to use.
3. Give priority to sustained compliance with all applicable environmental laws.
4. Continue to restore previously contaminated sites deemed as a threat to human health and the environment.[26]

By the end of the 1990s, the Army culture had changed sufficiently that environmental managers were well established in facility organizations, installations were routinely inspected for environmental compliance, and field commanders were so conscious of environmental details in their operations that they required their soldiers as standard operating procedures to place drip pans beneath their vehicles when in the field.

In the new century, the Department of Defense has undergone a "sea change . . . concerning environmental responsibility, moving beyond rote compliance with environmental laws and regulations toward total integration of environmental, safety and occupational health concerns into daily military operations, as well as long-term planning," wrote Alex Beehler, Assistant Deputy Undersecretary of Defense for Environment, Safety, and Occupational Health, and Air Force Lieutenant Colonel Ann Erin Mercer.[27] But that "sea change" was accompanied by efforts to seek legislative changes that would grant relief from certain environmental requirements for DOD activities—efforts that have brought stiff opposition from environmental groups but that also have been moderately successful in Congress.

When dealing with the military and the rest of the federal government under environmental and natural resources law, certain special issues often arise regarding environmental regulation and environmental planning. In many respects, the military does enjoy legal advantages over private sector entities. In other ways, such as compliance with the National Environmental Policy Act,[28] the military, as a part of the federal government, must follow special environmental procedures that are not applicable in the private sector. This can create a perplexing problem for state environmental regulators and the public, who wish only to ensure that environmental requirements are carried out equally by all entities. It appears to be a matter of simple fairness to hold federal agencies accountable for their actions as all other entities. If environmental activists and practitioners can gain an understanding of those common issues, it serves to demystify the special body of environmental law that applies to the federal government.

Notes

1. Stephen Dycus, National Defense and the Environment 1 (1996).
2. See testimony of Henry Habicht III, then Assistant Attorney General for the Land and Natural Resources Division, Department of Justice, in a hearing before the Subcommittee on Oversight and Investigations of the House Committee on Energy and Commerce, 100th Cong., 1st Sess., 210 (1987).
3. Exec. Order No. 12,088, 43 Fed. Reg. 47707 (1978).
4. See, e.g., Thomas Kearns, *An Examination of, and Suggested Revisions to, CERCLA's Provisions Waiving the Federal Government's Sovereign Immunity from Actions based on State Law*, 4 Buff. Envtl. L.J. 17 (1997); and Elizabeth Cheng, *Lawmaker as Lawbreaker: Assessing Civil Penalties against Federal Facilities under RCRA*, U. Chi. L. Rev. 845 (1990).
5. Kyle Bettigole, *Comment: Defending against Defense: Civil Resistance, Necessity and the United States Military's Toxic Legacy*, 21 B.C. Envtl. Aff. L. Rev. 667, 667–68(1994) (quoting from National Toxic Campaign Fund, *The U.S. Military's Toxic Legacy* I [1991]).
6. United States v. Dee, 912 F.2d 741, 743 (4th Cir. 1990).
7. 42 U.S.C. §§ 6901–92k.
8. *Dee*, 912 F.2d at 743.
9. *Id.* at 744.
10. *Id.* at 745.
11. Margaret Minister, *Federal Facilities and the Deterrence Failure of Environmental Laws: The Case for Criminal Prosecution of Federal Employees*, 18 Harv. Envtl. L. Rev. 137, 139 (1994).
12. *Id.* at 140.
13. 42 U.S.C. §§ 9601–75.

14. Minister, *Federal Facilities*, supra note 11, at 156.

15. *Id.* at 182.

16. 28 C.F.R. § 50.15(a).

17. *Id.* § 50.15(a)(4).

18. *Id.* § 50.15(a)(5).

19. *Id.* § 50.15(12)(b)(2).

20. *Id.* § 50.16.

21. Convention on the Prohibition of the Development, Production, Stockpiling and Use of Chemical Weapons and on Their Destruction, Paris, January 13, 1993, International Committee for the Red Cross website, www.icrc.org/ihl.nsf/385ec082b509e76c41256739003e636d/3f233cb0f0c580f8c125641f002d42a8?OpenDocument (accessed Sept. 3, 2006).

22. See *Families Concerned about Nerve Gas Incineration v. Army*, 380 F. Supp. 2d 1233 (N.D. Ala. 2005).

23. Statement presented by Hon. Jim Saxton, hearing before the Subcommittee on Terrorism, Unconventional Threats and Capabilities, 108th Cong., October 30, 2003, http://commdocs.house.gov/committees/security/has303260.000/has303260_0.HTM (accessed September 3, 2006).

24. U.S. Department of Energy, *DOE Certifies Rocky Flats Cleanup "Complete,"* Department of Energy website, www.energy.gov/news/2790.htm (accessed June 15, 2006).

25. Department of the Army, U.S. Army Corps of Engineers, Reg. 200-3-1 (2004).

26. Department of the Army, Reg. 200-1, 1 (1997).

27. Alex Beehler and Ann Erin Mercer, *Sea Change at Defense*, Envtl. Forum 21 (Sept./Oct. 2005).

28. 42 U.S.C. §§ 4321–70f.

2

Regulating the Military at Peace

WHILE MANY MIGHT ARGUE THAT ENVIRONMENTAL COMPLIANCE at military facilities is less than it should be, there is no question that environmental laws do apply to the military, at least to some degree. With a few exceptions, the military services must comply with environmental laws within the United States. Most important perhaps to the public is compliance with laws protecting the air we breathe and the water we drink. Certain environmental statutes, the laws that control pollution, are more closely related to these objectives. While the federal government, including the military, is required to comply with laws regulating pollution, there are some significant issues that state environmental officials should understand. Only then can state regulators effectively enforce state environmental law against federal agencies.

Civil Penalties and Sovereign Immunity

The principle of sovereign immunity is perhaps the most misunderstood of the special issues that arise in environmental regulation of the federal government's activities. It is regarded with disgust and frustration by many in the environmental community.[1] Under the sovereign immunity principle, only Congress can waive the federal government's immunity to lawsuits. States may regulate activities of federal agencies only when authorized to do so by Congress, and that authorization must be "clear and unambiguous."[2] However, each of the major environmental statutes provides a limited waiver of sovereign immunity that requires federal facilities to comply with state laws.[3] Normally, federal and state regulators have broad power to enforce pollution control requirements. If a facility violates any of the numerous pollution standards, then the regulators have several civil remedies at their disposal, including injunctive relief.[4] The waivers of sovereign immunity, however, generally have not given states the power to fine federal facilities, although state attorneys general have contended that the waivers do allow states to assess fines, or civil penalties, against the federal government. The Supreme Court's decision in *Department of Energy v. Ohio* reinforced the view that sovereign immunity waivers may not include civil penalties.[5] In dicta, however, the Court opined that some circumstances could arise under which the Clean Water Act (CWA) waiver might allow for civil penalties as "coercive sanctions."[6]

In 1992, however, Congress adopted the Federal Facilities Compliance Act (FFCA), which amended the Solid Waste Disposal Act (SWDA)—commonly known as the Resource Conservation and Recovery Act (RCRA)—allowing states to assess civil penalties against federal installations for noncompliance.[7] The FFCA, however, applied only to solid and hazardous waste.[8] The FFCA's waiver of sovereign immunity did not apply to any other environmental statutes.[9] Congress, however, has since passed similar legislation for the lead exposure amendments to the Toxic Substance Control Act (TSCA)[10] and the Safe Drinking Water Act (SDWA).[11]

The underlying premise supporting sovereign immunity originates from the Supremacy Clause of the U.S. Constitution and is "exemplified in the Plenary Powers Clause of the Constitution."[12] The principle established that states could not constitutionally regulate federal activities unless Congress consented to such regulation. Congress, however, has not always crafted clear sovereign immunity language. Therefore, courts have developed rules of interpretation when sovereign immunity was claimed based on ambiguous language.[13] The rules of interpretation—outlined in *McClellan Ecological Seepage Situation (MESS) v. Weinberger*—concluded that a waiver of sovereign immunity would not be recognized unless it was "clear, concise and unequivocal."[14] Further, "If there is any doubt, waiver will not be found. Waiver cannot be implied. It cannot be assumed. It cannot be based on speculation, surmise or conjecture."[15] This premise later was reiterated in the Supreme Court's opinion in *Department of Energy v. Ohio*, in which the Court determined that the Department of Energy could not be fined for past violations of the RCRA or the CWA.[16]

The doctrine of sovereign immunity has a long history. With regard to environmental statutes, the Supreme Court's 1976 decision in *Hancock v. Train* prompted a new legislative trend toward more clearly worded waivers of sovereign immunity.[17] In that case, the Supreme Court held that the state permitting requirements did not apply to federal installations. Congress responded by amending the federal facility provisions of the Clean Air Act (CAA), the CWA, and the SDWA and passed a more carefully worded sovereign immunity waiver with the RCRA.[18] The waiver language in these environmental statutes, although similar, is not uniform. Therefore, practitioners must carefully examine each waiver separately to fully understand its applications.

Section 313(a) of the CWA, for instance, requires federal installations to "comply with all Federal, State, Interstate, and local requirements, administrative authority, and process and sanctions respecting the control and abatement of water pollution in the same manner, and to the same extent as any nongovernmental entity including the payment of reasonable service charges."[19] Following the Supreme Court's decision in *Hancock v. Train*, Congress added that the waiver "shall apply (A) to any requirement whether substantive or procedural (including any recordkeeping or reporting requirement, any requirement respecting permits and any other requirement, whatsoever)."[20] The section further waives immunity "to any process and sanction, whether enforced in Federal, State, or local courts or in any other manner."[21] The CWA waiver also provides that the federal government may remove any sanction against it to federal district court and that no officer or employee of the federal government could be held liable for fines arising from "performance of his official duties."[22] Finally, the "United States shall be liable only for those civil penalties arising under Federal law or imposed by State or local court to enforce an order or the process of such court."[23]

In *Department of Energy v. Ohio*, the Court's decision on the CWA sovereign immunity waiver hinged, among other things, on the interpretation of the term "process and sanctions."[24] The State of Ohio had sought penalties for violations of state and federal pollution laws—including the CWA and the RCRA—at the Department of Energy's uranium processing plant in Fernald, Ohio.[25] The state contended that the "federal facilities" and "citizen-suit" sections in the CWA effectively waived sovereign immunity for fines. Ohio argued that the word "sanction" in the CWA federal facilities section was intended to encompass punitive fines.[26] The Supreme Court, however, held that any waiver of sovereign immunity must be clear and unequivocal and—with regard to punitive fines—the CWA sovereign immunity waiver failed to meet that test.[27]

The Court also opined that states could impose civil penalties if assessed as "coercive sanctions."[28] Justice David Souter wrote for the majority that the language in the CWA waiver that federal facilities "shall be subject to . . . all Federal, State and local . . . sanctions" indicated that Congress intended to allow civil penalties when used as a coercive tool in instruments such as court orders or judgments.[29] Justice Souter also found support for this interpretation of the language that the "United States shall be liable only for those civil penalties arising under Federal law or imposed by a State or local court to enforce an order or the process of such court."[30] The *Department of Energy v. Ohio* dictum indicates that, under the CWA waiver, local courts might be able to issue compliance orders followed by contempt citations for violations, and possibly even stipulated penalties. The latter passage is unique to the CWA. Therefore, a state seeking "coercive sanctions" pursuant to any other environmental statute would be less likely to succeed.

Some commentators reacted harshly to the Court's decision in *Department of Energy v. Ohio.* One commentator saw its requirement of a "clear and unequivocal waiver" as part of a pattern by the Court of establishing "clear statement rules" in many contexts. "The Court has not explained why it created such a strong clear statement rule for waivers of federal sovereign immunity," wrote Professor John C. Nagle. "None of the Court's opinions have defended sovereign immunity or explained the apparently increased need to protect the federal government from suit."[31] The undeniable result of the case, however, was to put the responsibility for drafting a clear statement back on Congress. Although Congress may originally have intended that civil penalties be among states' enforcement tools against the federal government, following *Department of Energy v. Ohio* they no longer were.

In response to *Department of Energy v. Ohio*, Congress significantly altered the reach of sovereign immunity under RCRA by passage of the FFCA.[32] Under the FFCA, state and federal regulators clearly can assess fines against federal facilities for violating solid and hazardous waste laws. In its present form, the federal facilities provision of the RCRA provides that the federal government be subject to "all administrative orders and all civil and administrative penalties and fines, regardless of whether such penalties or fines are punitive or coercive in nature or are imposed for isolated, intermittent, or continuing violations."[33] Furthermore, "The United States hereby expressly waives any immunity otherwise applicable to the United States with respect to any such substantive or procedural requirement (including, but not limited to, any injunctive relief, administrative order or civil or administrative penalty or fine referred to in the preceding sentence, or reasonable service charge)."[34] With the FFCA, Congress rendered obsolete any case law holding that the RCRA waiver of sovereign immunity was not "clear and unequivocal." The FFCA also clarified the meaning of "reasonable service charge" to include charges in connection with processing necessary paperwork "as well as any other nondiscriminatory charges that are assessed in connection with a . . . solid or hazardous waste regulatory program."[35] The FFCA also created a second subsection that empowers the Environmental Protection Agency to initiate administrative actions against federal facilities.[36] While the FFCA states that the federal government would be liable for RCRA violations "for isolated, intermittent, or continuing violations," federal facilities still have a defense against actions for past violations. President George H. W. Bush, in his adoption press release, stated his belief that the FFCA was ratified "notwithstanding the holding of the Supreme Court in *Gwaltney of Smithfield, Ltd. v. Chesapeake Bay Foundation*."[37] In *Gwaltney*, the Court held that the Chesapeake Bay Foundation could not compel the meat-packer defendant to pay civil penalties for wholly past permit violations but rather was required to allege that such violations were likely to continue.[38]

Additionally, federal agencies, in particular the Department of Defense, argued that the FFCA, by its own language, only applied to solid and hazardous waste regulation—that it did not apply to any other environmental laws, such as the RCRA sections governing underground storage tanks (USTs).[39] Section 9007 of the RCRA provides its own waiver of sovereign immunity governing USTs that is comparable to other sovereign immunity waivers in substance and scope.[40] The agencies argued that Section 9007 provided the exclusive waiver of sovereign immunity for UST regulation. The U.S. Environmental Protection Agency (EPA), however, began assessing penalties against federal facilities in 1998 for failure to meet UST compliance deadlines. The Department of Defense requested an opinion from the Office of Legal Counsel (OLC), Department of Justice, to clarify the issue. In an opinion dated June 14, 2000, the OLC concluded "that RCRA clearly grants EPA the authority to assess penalties against federal agencies for UST violations."[41] Without relying on the FFCA waiver of sovereign immunity as authority, the OLC determined that Section 9006(a)(1) of Subtitle I of the RCRA gave the EPA authority to issue administrative compliance orders to "any person."[42] Further, OLC found that Section 9006(c) gave the EPA authority to "assess a penalty, if any, which the Administrator determines is reasonable taking into account the seriousness of the violation and any good faith efforts to comply with the applicable requirements."[43] Under Section 9001 of RCRA, the definition of "person" includes "the United States Government."[44] Further, the OLC determined that, while the FFCA may have given states authority only to assess civil penalties for hazardous or solid waste violations, the federal facilities provision of the RCRA gave the EPA Administrator broader authority to assess fines against federal agencies.[45]

Until recently, federal agencies would have continued to resist civil penalties assessed by states under UST regulations because the FFCA and the OLC opinion did not specifically address state penalties for USTs. In its previous version, the waiver of sovereign immunity for USTs[46] was similar to other non-RCRA sovereign immunity waivers. As with other federal facilities sections, Congress had waived sovereign immunity against "all Federal, State, interstate, and local requirements" for USTs.[47] Section 9007, however, did not waive sovereign immunity explicitly against "process and sanctions," as do the other environmental sovereign immunity waivers.[48] The only mention of "process or sanction" in the waiver was in regard to injunctive remedies.[49] Therefore, Justice Souter's dictum in *Department of Energy v. Ohio*—indicating that states could impose civil penalties under the CWA if imposed as "coercive sanctions"—could not have been construed to allow stipulated penalties for USTs. Accordingly, based on that case, a state could not have made a credible argument for stipulated penalties regarding USTs. The 2005 Energy Policy Act, however, provided for a clear waiver of sovereign immunity to include "all civil and administrative penalties and fines"[50] for violations of UST requirements. (Arguably, the absence of the "process and sanction" language in the UST sovereign immunity waiver until 2005 represented sound public policy. The UST amendment regulates USTs that may have been placed in the ground many years ago. As with the Comprehensive Environmental Response, Compensation, and Liability Act [CERCLA or Superfund],[51] the UST amendments primarily address and attempt to correct already-existing conditions, rather than being a prospective compliance program as the other statutes are. During the 1990s, most federal facilities upgraded USTs on their grounds to meet required standards. By waiting until 2005 to provide for civil penalties, Congress allowed federal agencies to accomplish UST upgrades without the potential for being fined for conditions that predated passage of the UST amendments.)

Further, the FFCA applies only to environmental laws aimed at regulating solid and hazardous wastes. For example, the sovereign immunity principle traditionally has included exemption from local building codes and zoning ordinances.[52] Therefore, if a local government attempts to limit a federal facility's solid waste activities, such as landfills, through zoning restrictions, sovereign immunity still would exempt the activity despite the FFCA because local governments lack zoning jurisdiction on federal enclaves.

As with the CWA, the federal government under Section 118 of the CAA is required to comply with "all Federal, State, interstate and local requirements, administrative authority, and process and sanctions" regarding air pollution "in the same manner, and to the same extent, as any nongovernmental entity."[53] With regard to payment of fines under the CAA, however, there is a split of authority in the federal courts that has yet to be resolved. Although the language of the CAA waiver of sovereign immunity is substantially similar to the language the Court considered in *Department of Energy v. Ohio*, the Sixth Circuit held that the CAA's savings clause in its citizen suit provision contains an independent waiver of sovereign immunity authorizing state-imposed punitive civil fines.[54] In contrast, the Eleventh Circuit held that the Supreme Court's interpretation in *Department of Energy v. Ohio* of similar federal facility section language was controlling.[55]

Because CERCLA is not primarily a compliance statute in the nature of the CWA, the CAA, and the RCRA, the federal facilities section of CERCLA operates substantially differently than the other environmental statutes.[56] Pursuant to CERCLA Section 120, federal facilities are liable for hazardous waste cleanup costs for which they are responsible.[57] Unlike other statutes, there is no clear waiver of sovereign immunity for state "administrative enforcement authority."[58] Under Executive Order 12,580, federal lead authority for CERCLA cleanup at DOD installations has been delegated to the military services themselves.[59] The Defense agencies carry out their environmental cleanup efforts pursuant to the Defense Environmental Restoration Program (DERP),[60] incorporating state requirements as "applicable or relevant and appropriate requirements" and coordinating with state regulators under Defense-State Memorandums of Agreement (DSMOAs).[61] But the military services do not view state environmental officers as regulators for CERCLA akin to regulators of other environmental regimes.

Thus, state regulators appear to lack enforcement authority under CERCLA to issue orders to compel military services to conduct cleanups of contamination on federal property. While the federal government may be sued as a party that is partially responsible for the release of hazardous substances, no provision for punitive fines exists. Stipulated penalties, however, arguably could be included in a consent decree that would set cleanup milestones.[62] Under CERCLA's enforcement section, stipulated penalties of up to $25,000 per day may be included in a consent decree.[63] However, a federal agency could still argue that Congress has not "clearly and unequivocally" waived sovereign immunity for state regulation—to include any economic sanctions.

One way in which state regulators can creatively hold federal facilities accountable, especially in situations in which punitive fines are questionable, would be through the use of supplemental environmental projects (SEPs). Under SEPs, a federal facility may agree to establish proactive environmental programs in lieu of penalties. This approach is often better for the environment and can avoid contentious wrangling over applicability of punitive fines, although the federal agency may resist agreeing to SEPs if it is well established under an environmental statute that there is no waiver of sovereign immunity for civil penalties. If an agreement for a SEP can be reached, however, it avoids the questionable public policy of fining one taxpayer-funded agency by another.[64]

Sovereign Immunity and Applicability of State Law

Under the principle of sovereign immunity, federal environmental attorneys may also contend that certain state regulatory schemes are completely inapplicable to federal activities. Such issues are emerging now between state regulators and federal agencies, with the federal agencies contending that the scope of each environmental waiver of sovereign immunity is limited to the scope of the federal law. Numerous cases, for instance, have held that the CWA does not apply to groundwater.[65] Therefore, federal agencies can argue that the waiver of sovereign immunity under the CWA does not apply to groundwater regulation by states[66] unless those regulations fall under the sovereign immunity waiver under the Safe Drinking Water Act, which is restricted by the scope of the Act to underground injection and wellhead protection.[67]

Further, depending on applicable facts, federal agencies may argue that state aboveground storage tank regulatory programs are inapplicable because there is no federal counterpart and therefore no waiver of sovereign immunity. However, this argument would be limited to unique circumstances involving closed basins not connected to "waters of the United States."[68] State regulators do have authority under the CWA to regulate ASTs that may release into waters of the United States.[69] But absent authority under the UST provisions and absent a potential for a release into waters of the United States, states may lack a legal hook with which to regulate the ASTs.

Federal agencies have also contended that the waiver of sovereign immunity in RCRA does not provide state regulators the authority to compel the agencies to surrender a property right.[70] Under state law, for instance, Colorado requires an "environmental covenant" for any environmental remediation project in which residual environmental contamination would be left in place that would require some land use restrictions to be placed on the property.[71] The environmental covenant is a recorded instrument containing applicable environmental use restrictions.[72] It cannot be "extinguished, limited, or impaired through issuance of a tax deed or through adverse possession, nor may an environmental covenant be extinguished, limited, or impaired by reason of the doctrines of abandonment, waiver, lack of enforcement, or other common law principles relating to covenants, or by the exercise of eminent domain."[73] Under Colorado law, the environmental covenant "shall run with the land and shall bind the owner of the land, the owner's successors and assigns, and any person using the land."[74] Although there are significant potential benefits to placing such environmental covenants on properties, federal agencies have been reluctant to concede to state authority to partially condemn federal property interests. This issue is of particular significance with regard to base realignment and closure (BRAC) property and will be discussed further in chapter 6.

Similarly, there are circumstances under which the CERCLA and the RCRA corrective action provisions would both apply. Under Section 120 of CERCLA and Executive Order 12,580, federal agencies are essentially self-regulating in environmental cleanup actions at non–National Priorities List (NPL) sites. At NPL sites, the EPA has primacy under CERCLA and arguably should preempt state regulation. Although in essence a federal preemption argument rather than a sovereign immunity argument, federal agencies have argued that exclusive regulatory authority over NPL sites should rest in the United States. However, in *United States v. Colorado*,[75] the Tenth Circuit upheld Colorado's right to enforce its RCRA authority on the Rocky Mountain Arsenal, an NPL site. The court held that even though the Arsenal was listed on the NPL, the state's RCRA corrective action order did not constitute an impermissible challenge to the ongoing CERCLA remedial action.[76]

Payment of Reasonable Fees

Each of the federal facilities provisions of the environmental statutes provides that federal facilities have waived sovereign immunity to pay "reasonable" administrative fees or service charges.[77] Pursuant to the Supremacy Clause of the Constitution, however, the federal government would not normally pay taxes to the state.[78] (An exception is disposal of federal low-level radioactive waste at nonfederal disposal facilities, which is subject to "fees, taxes and surcharges").[79] The federal government cannot be compelled to pay a state tax without a clear "congressional mandate."[80] Many "fees" that military facilities are requested to pay are couched in terminology that does not make it evident whether they are really fees that can be paid, or, instead, taxes that cannot. This question arises routinely on military installations when state regulators process invoices for annual environmental fees. Such fees may include labels such as "hazardous waste management fees," "water pollution fees," and "fees for environmental services." Fees are charges for services rendered by state or local government regulators as a part of the administration of environmental programs. To determine whether a charge is payable as a "fee" or must not be paid because it is a "tax," federal government attorneys have relied on the three-prong test set forth in *Massachusetts v. United States*.[81] Under the *Massachusetts* analysis, the attorney would determine first whether the charge is nondiscriminatory in its application[82]—that is, whether the charge disproportionately would penalize the federal agency as compared with nonfederal entities. Second, the attorney would determine whether the charge was a fair approximation of the "benefits" the facility received from the state.[83] If the charge was for some service for which the federal government was not eligible, for instance, such as a remediation fund for leaking USTs, then the federal government could not pay the fee. Finally, the federal attorney would determine if the charge was structured to produce revenues that would not exceed the total cost to the state of providing the benefits to be supplied. If a state charged a fee that produced revenue for the general revenue fund for use in other programs, then it was considered a tax, and the federal agency would not pay it.[84]

But the federal environmental attorney's framework for analysis of environmental fees was altered somewhat by a 2006 comptroller general opinion.[85] Under the comptroller general's decision, the U.S. Forest Service was informed that surface water management fees assessed against national forest lands by King County, Washington, constituted a tax and were not payable under the CWA's waiver of sovereign immunity.[86] The services provided by the county in exchange for payment of the "fee" would have included "basin planning, facilities maintenance, regulation, financial administration, public involvement, drainage investigation and enforcement, aquatic resource restoration, surface and storm water quality and environmental monitoring, natural surface water drainage system planning, intergovernmental relations, and facility design and construction."[87] In its analysis of the King County "fee," the comptroller general found the *Massachusetts* test to be "inapposite" to determining federal immunity from state taxation. The comptroller general instead applied the three-part test from *San Juan Cellular Tel. Co. v. Public Service Comm'n of Puerto Rico*[88] to determine whether the King County charge was a "classic" tax. Under the *San Juan Cellular* test, as summarized by the comptroller general, a tax is a charge that "(1) is imposed by a legislature upon many, or all, citizens, (2) raises money, and (3) is spent for the benefit of the entire community."[89] A fee, on the other hand, "is imposed by an agency upon those subject to its regulation, may serve regulatory purposes, and may raise money to be placed in a special fund to help defray the agency's regulation-related expenses."[90] In ambiguous cases, the purpose of the charge may be determinative. "When the three-part inquiry yields a result that places the charge somewhere in the middle of the *San Juan Cellular* description, that is, when assessments have characteristics of both 'taxes' and 'fees,' the most important factor becomes the purpose behind the statute or regulation that imposes the charge," the comptroller general wrote. "In those circumstances, if the ultimate use of the revenue benefits the general public, then the charge will qualify as a 'tax,' while if the benefits are more narrowly circumscribed, then the charge will more likely qualify as a 'fee.'"[91]

Environmental Protection Overseas

Much of the peacetime force of the United States has been sailing the seas and has been stationed in foreign nations during the past several decades. Naval vessels in international waters must comply with international maritime law, including the International Convention for the Prevention of Pollution from Ships.[92] On land, there is generally no direct application of U.S. environmental law at peacetime military installations overseas.[93] When operating on foreign soil, U.S. forces will be required to comply with agreements negotiated with host nations, which are known as Status of Forces Agreements (SOFAs). In addition, there is a DOD directive that requires the services to follow, at a minimum, "baseline" environmental standards applicable to similar operations in the United States.[94] Waivers from applicable standards are granted only after consultation with the U.S. diplomatic mission in the nation and are limited to situations in which "compliance with the standards at particular installations or facilities would seriously impair their actions, adversely affect relations with the host nation or would require substantial expenditure of funds for physical improvements at an installation that has been identified for closure or . . . realignment."[95] Disposal of hazardous wastes overseas are limited to instances in which either (1) disposal complies with the baseline guidance and any applicable SOFA or (2) disposal complies with the baseline guidance, and host nation authorities have otherwise agreed to the disposal.[96] A document establishing the "baseline" for environmental compliance overseas was published by DOD in March 2000.[97]

But while the baseline standards might meet substantive requirements of host nations, they might not completely satisfy host environmental regulators. In a report issued November 14, 2000, the DOD inspector general issued a report concluding that the military services were generally in compliance with "country-specific final governing standards" within the European Command.[98] In Italy, however, DOD civilian personnel were charged with Italian hazardous waste procedural and administrative violations and levied fines. The report concluded that "the violations occurred because DOD policy does not recognize host nation procedural and administrative requirements as applicable environmental standards, and no interim guidance was provided as to how to respond to Italian regulatory enforcement actions."[99]

Notes

1. See, e.g., Thomas Kearns, *An Examination of, and Suggested Revisions to, CERCLA's Provisions Waiving the Federal Government's Sovereign Immunity from Actions based on State Law*, 4 Buff. Envtl. L.J. 17 (1997); and Elizabeth Cheng, *Lawmaker as Lawbreaker: Assessing Civil Penalties against Federal Facilities under RCRA*, U. Chi. L. Rev. 845 (1990).

2. Environmental Protection Agency v. California *ex rel.* State Water Resources Control Bd., 426 U.S. 200, 211 (1976).

3. See, e.g., 42 U.S.C. § 300j-6; 33 U.S.C. § 1323; 42 U.S.C. § 6961; 42 U.S.C. § 7418.

4. See, e.g., 33 U.S.C. § 1323.

5. Department of Energy v. Ohio, 503 U.S. 607, 615 (1992).

6. *Id.* at 615–20.

7. Federal Facilities Compliance Act, Pub. L. No. 102-386, 106 Stat. 1505 (1992). The FFCA addressed not only sovereign immunity but also other federal government concerns, such as development of rules governing military munitions disposals (§ 107).

8. *Id.*

9. 42 U.S.C. § 6991f.

10. 15 U.S.C. § 2688.

11. 42 U.S.C. § 300j-6.

12. Lt. Col. Richard Lotz, *Federal Facility Provisions of Federal Environmental Statutes: Waiver of Sovereign Immunity for "Requirements" and Fines and Penalties*, 31 Air Force L. Rev. 7, 8 (1989) (citing *Hancock v. Train*, 426 U.S. 167 [1976]); see U.S. Const. art. 1, § 8, cl. 17.

13. *Id.*

14. *Id.*; see McClellan Ecological Seepage Situation v. Weinberger, 707 F. Supp. 1182, 1187 (E.D. Calif. 1988).

15. *McClellan Ecological Seepage Situation*, 707 F. Supp. at 1187.

16. *Ohio*, 503 U.S. at 615–29.

17. Lotz, *Federal Facility*, supra note 12, at 11.

18. *Id.*

19. 33 U.S.C. § 1323(a).

20. *Id.*

21. *Id.*

22. *Id.*

23. *Id.*

24. *Ohio*, 503 U.S. at 620–23.

25. *Id.* at 612.

26. *Id.* at 620.

27. *Id.* at 627.

28. *Id.* at 624.

29. *Id.* at 623–24.

30. *Id.* at 624.

31. John C. Nagle, *Waiving Sovereign Immunity in an Age of Clear Statement Rules*, 1995 Wis. L. Rev. 771, 774 (1995).

32. 42 U.S.C. § 6961.

33. *Id.*

34. *Id.*

35. *Id.*

36. *Id.*

37. President George H. W. Bush press release accompanying the signing of the FFCA (October 6, 1992).

38. Gwaltney of Smithfield, Ltd. v. Chesapeake Bay Found., 484 U.S. 49 (1987).

39. *Id.*

40. 42 U.S.C. § 6991f(a).

41. MEMORANDUM OPINION FOR THE GENERAL COUNSEL, DEPARTMENT OF DEFENSE, AND THE GENERAL COUNSEL, ENVIRONMENTAL PROTECTION AGENCY, *EPA Assessment of Penalties against Federal Agencies for Violation of the Underground Storage Tank Requirements of the Resource Conservation and Recovery Act,* June 14, 2000.

42. *Id.*, citing 42 U.S.C. § 6991e(a)(1).

43. *Id.*, citing 42 U.S.C. § 6991e(c).

44. *Id.*, citing 42 U.S.C. § 6991(6).

45. *Id.*, citing 42 U.S.C. § 6961(b)(1).

46. 42 U.S.C. § 6991f(1).

47. *Id.*

48. *Id.*

49. *Id.*

50. Pub. L. 109-58, Title XV, Subtitle B, § 1528, 119 Stat. 1100.

51. See 42 U.S.C. §§ 9601–75.

52. United States v. Chester, 144 F.2d 415 (3d Cir. 1944); *United States v. Philadelphia,* 56 F. Supp. 862 (E.D. Pa. 1944) *affd.*, 147 F.2d 291 (3d Cir.), *cert. denied,* 325 U.S. 870 (1945).

53. 42 U.S.C. § 7418.

54. United States v. Tennessee Air Pollution Control Board, No. 97-5715 (6th Cir. 1999).

55. City of Jacksonville v. Navy, 348 F.3d 1307 (11th Cir. 2003).

56. 42 U.S.C. § 9620(a)(1).

57. *Id.*

58. *Id.*

59. Exec. Order No. 12,580, § 2(d), 52 Fed. Reg. 2923 (1987).

60. 10 U.S.C. § 2701–8 and 2810.

61. See Final Department of Defense-State Memorandum of Agreement, www.epa.gov/swerffrr/documents/swp789.htm (accessed Nov. 11, 2005).

62. 42 U.S.C. § 9621.

63. *Id.*

64. In section 315 of the National Defense Authorization Act for 2001, for instance, Congress approved the expenditure of $993,000 for a hazardous substance management system at Walter Reed Army Medical Center in satisfaction of a fine imposed by the EPA. See, U.S. Army, ENVIRONMENTAL LAW DIVISION BULLETIN, Oct. 2000.

65. See, e.g., Rice v. Harken Exploration Co., 250 F.3d 392, 399 (5th Cir. 2001); Village of Oconomowoc Lake v. Dayton Hudson Corp., 24 F.3d 962, 965 (7th Cir. 1994).

66. Such as the New Mexico Ground and Surface Water Protection Regulations (20 NMAC § 6.2.1 et seq.).

67. 42 U.S.C. § 300j-6.

68. See 33 U.S.C. § 1362(7).

69. 33 U.S.C. §§ 1251–1387.

70. See Daniel Miller, *Looking a Gift Horse in the Mouth: Federal Agency Opposition to State Institutional Control Laws,* 32 ENVTL. L. REP. 11115 (2002).

71. Colo. Rev. Stat. § 25-15-319.

72. Colo. Rev. Stat. § 25-15-101.

73. Colo. Rev. Stat. § 25-15-318(1).

74. Colo. Rev. Stat. § 25-15-318(2).

75. United States v. Colorado, 990 F.2d 1565 (10th Cir. 1993), *cert. denied*, 510 U.S. 1092 (1994).

76. *Id.* at 1581–82.

77. See, e.g., 42 U.S.C. § 300j-6; 33 U.S.C. § 1323; 42 U.S.C. § 6961; 42 U.S.C. § 7418.

78. See Massachusetts v. United States, 435 U.S. 444 (1978); U.S. Const. art. 1, § 8, cl. 17.

79. 42 U.S.C. § 2021d(b)(1)(B).

80. Kern-Limerick, Inc. v. Scurlock, 347 U.S. 110, 122 (1954).

81. Massachusetts v. United States, 435 U.S. 444 (1978).

82. *Id.* at 454–63.

83. *Id.* at 463–67.

84. *Id.*

85. Matter of Forest Service—Surface Water Management Fees, 2006 U.S. Comp. Gen. LEXIS 93, July 5, 2006.

86. *Id.*

87. *Id.*

88. San Juan Cellular Tel. Co. v. Public Service Comm'n of Puerto Rico, 967 F.2d 683, 685 (1st Cir. 1992).

89. Matter of Forest Service, supra note 85.

90. *Id.*

91. *Id.*

92. The International Convention for the Prevention of Pollution from Ships (MARPOL) was adopted on November 2, 1973, and covered pollution by oil, chemicals, harmful substances in packaged form, sewage, and garbage. See www.imo.org/Conventions/contents.asp?doc_id=678&topic_id=258 (accessed Sept. 3, 2006).

93. An exception is application of National Environmental Policy Act requirements in Antarctica. Environmental Defense Fund v. Massey, 986 F.2d 528 (D.C. Cir. 1993).

94. Management of Environmental Compliance at overseas Installations, Department of Defense Instruction (DODI) 4715.5, Apr. 22, 1996.

95. Id. § 6.6.

96. Id. § 6.4.

97. Overseas Environmental Baseline Guidance Documant (OEBGD) (DOD 47 1 5.5-G), Mar. 15, 2000, www.denix.osd.mil/denix/Public/Library/Intl/OEBGD/toc.html (accessed Oct. 25, 2005).

98. Inspector General, Department of Defense, Evaluation Report: DOD Compliance with Hazardous Waste Laws in the U.S. European Command, Report No. D-2001-009 at 4, Nov. 14, 2000.

99. *Id.*

3

Environmental Planning at Military Facilities

THE MILITARY AND OTHER FEDERAL AGENCIES do indeed follow their own set of rules with respect to environmental law. In some cases, sovereign immunity might provide a shield to regulation under state law. Some of the federal agencies' regulations, however, are significantly more stringent than regulations that apply to any state or private entities. Environmental planning regulations, for instance, afford the public and state and local governments an opportunity to shape federal programs and projects at their inception. When dealing with the federal government in the arena of environmental and natural resources law, practitioners must understand the unique array of requirements involved in federal facility environmental planning.

The National Environmental Policy Act

The major environmental planning statute is the National Environmental Policy Act (NEPA). NEPA requires that federal agencies analyze the effects of an action on the environment when taking any "major Federal action significantly affecting the quality of the human environment."[1] The implementing regulations, developed by the White House Council on Environmental Quality (CEQ), establish rules for conducting the type of environmental analysis required for a given activity or project.[2] Federal agencies have further elaborated on those regulations by adopting their own regulations.[3]

An agency must prepare different types of NEPA documentation depending on the level of environmental impact that is possible. If an action or project definitely will not have an adverse impact on the environment, no NEPA documentation or only minimal NEPA documentation will be required.[4] If an action or project could possibly cause significant environmental impacts, the agency must prepare at least an environmental assessment (EA).[5] An EA is intended to evaluate whether significant environmental effects would likely occur as a result of an activity or project.[6] The EA can help the agency to determine whether to conduct an environmental impact statement (EIS), but an EA is not a prerequisite to an EIS.[7] If an agency activity or project will have a significant impact on the quality of the environment, then the agency must definitely prepare an EIS.[8]

Each federal agency has a number of "categorical exclusions," established under agency regulations, for which NEPA environmental documentation is not required. These categorical exclusions consist of routine actions, such as routine maintenance and repair, which the participating agencies have determined do not affect the environment either as an individual project or when considered in light of other projects. The use of such categorical exclusions is encouraged under the CEQ regulations.[9] An EA is appropriate if a categorical exclusion does not apply to a proposed action or project and if some minor environmental damage could occur.[10]

If an EA is completed and it results in a "finding of no significant impact (FNSI)," then NEPA requires no further environmental analysis. If the proposed action would cause significant environmental impact, however, the agency must conduct an EIS, which is the highest level of environmental analysis.[11] In addition, an agency can complete a higher level of analysis on a project than is required. Conducting an EIS allows a federal agency to prepare and to present matters regarding controversial proposals. In a few select circumstances, an agency may also determine that, although completing an EIS would not be legally necessary, it would be prudent to conduct the EIS for strategic purposes, such as to garner public support for a proposed action or project.[12]

Major federal actions that will have an effect on the environment require NEPA documentation.[13] Which projects constitute "major federal actions" that will have an effect on the "environment," however, can be a matter of contention. "Major federal actions" can include rule-making or licensing decisions that can affect the environment indirectly.[14] Whether a proposed action requires an EIS is not always obvious. Projects that affect the environment have included a proposed low-income housing project on Manhattan's Upper West Side[15] and a proposed jail adjacent to the federal courthouse in New York City.[16] In considering a court challenge to the proposed federal jail in New York City, the U.S. Court of Appeals for the Second Circuit determined that NEPA requires a federal agency to consider at least two factors when analyzing the environmental impacts of a proposed action: "(1) the extent to which the action will cause adverse environmental effects in excess of those created by existing uses in the area affected by it, and (2) the absolute quantitative adverse environmental effects of the action itself, including the cumulative harm that results from its contribution to existing adverse conditions or uses in the affected area."[17]

Determining whether an EA or an EIS is sufficient is highly subjective. To ensure that the documents in either the EA or the EIS are adequate, a federal agency environmental attorney will review each document and determine whether it meets the requirements of the CEQ regulations. For instance, the document must always present an analysis of all reasonable alternatives, including a "no action" alternative, not just the proposed action.[18] The document must also indicate that the agency proponent considered the issue of environmental justice—that is, whether minority or low-income populations disproportionately suffer negative effects as a result of the proposed action.[19]

The agency must apply NEPA during the planning process prior to making any project decisions.[20] If an agency makes a decision prior to applying NEPA and uses an EA or an EIS for a post hoc rationalization of its decision, the agency's action is illegal and vulnerable to a lawsuit. Under the CEQ regulations, an agency cannot take action on a project that will "limit the choice of reasonable alternatives."[21] Thus, any action on a project that would predispose a federal agency toward a particular decision, such as awarding a contract to begin preparation work, makes the action vulnerable to a lawsuit.

A common error federal project proponents make in preparation of an EA or EIS is "segmentation," or "piecemealing," which is the practice of dividing a single action "into component parts, each involving actions with less significant environmental effects."[22] "Segmentation" or "piecemealing" would occur if an agency analyzed different phases of a single project as separate projects in separate EAs to avoid conducting an EIS on the total project. Separately analyzing a separate and distinct project, however, is legal and proper. In addition, "tiering" is also proper and encouraged in the CEQ regulations.[23] When some or most of the aspects of a proposed action have already been discussed in an earlier EIS, it is permissible to tier off that earlier document with a more succinct environmental analysis to avoid "repetitive discussions" of the same issues.[24] An EIS can also incorporate by reference information from other documents.[25] If an agency chooses to produce an EIS for a proposal, however, it need not be tiered off another EIS because an EIS, by definition and practice, is a complete analysis of an action.

Beyond the rudimentary requirements, the better and more complete an EA or EIS is, the more likely it is that the federal proponent agency will prevail in a court challenge. Federal agencies must apply a "rule of reason" to determine what factors to analyze. Mere speculation or "worst case" analysis is not required.[26] The purpose of the process is to ensure that federal agencies consider the environmental effects of their planned projects and actions. Agencies must "give serious weight to environmental factors" when making project decisions.[27] An "affected party" who notices a defect or deficiency in an EA or an EIS may have a legal cause of action. The Supreme Court early on recognized that NEPA creates a right of action to sue to enforce federal agency obligations to consider environmental impacts of their actions.[28] As a result, NEPA is a ripe area for litigation against the federal government and a means of holding it accountable. State officials and the public can make use of a federal agency's NEPA requirements to ensure that all potential environmental impacts of a project are considered.

In an emergency situation, a military service can seek to apply the alternative procedures policy allowed under the CEQ regulations.[29] The alternative procedures, however, are not intended to excuse the agency completely from its NEPA analysis responsibility. Under the emergency provision, the agency must consult with the CEQ, and the agency and CEQ "will limit such arrangements to actions necessary to control the immediate impacts of the emergency. Other actions remain subject to NEPA review."[30] This emergency procedure has been applied and upheld by federal courts in wartime circumstances, such as ramping up the rate of flights departing from Westover Air Force Base in Massachusetts during Operations Desert Shield and Desert Storm and during the demobilization from those overseas situations.[31]

The Endangered Species Act

Endangered Species Act (ESA)[32] compliance will often occur in concert with the NEPA process. Section 7 of ESA requires that federal agencies consult with the U.S. Fish and Wildlife Service[33] to determine whether a proposed activity or project will subject any threatened or endangered species or its critical habitat to "jeopardy."[34] When a federal agency proposes "major construction"[35] (or other activities having a similar impact on the environment) in an area where species included on the Endangered Species List are present, it must prepare a "biological assessment."[36] The U.S. Fish and Wildlife Service will prepare a "biological opinion" that analyzes whether a threatened or endangered species (or critical habitat) is jeopardized by the proposed project or activity.[37] The Service must determine whether the proposed project or activity will jeopardize threatened or endangered species (or result in the destruction or adverse modification of critical habitat) or whether an "incidental take"[38] will result that would jeopardize an endangered species.[39] The Service will issue a biological opinion (BO) that describes the effects on the species, describes reasonable and prudent measures to minimize harm to the species, and sets forth terms with which the proponent agency must comply to implement its proposed action.[40] If, after consultation, however, the Service still determines that the activity will "jeopardize" the species, a "jeopardy opinion" will result.[41]

Although there is a process for obtaining an exemption from endangered species requirements for an agency action,[42] a finding by the U.S. Fish and Wildlife Service that an agency action would place a listed species in jeopardy will normally terminate the proposed action. In *Tennessee Valley Authority v. Hill*,[43] a tiny minnow-like fish, the snail darter, shut down the massive Tellico Dam project. In the Supreme Court's opinion, Justice Warren Burger wrote, "it may be curious to some that the survival of a relatively small number of three-inch fish among all the countless millions of species extant would require the permanent halting of a virtually completed dam for which Congress has expended more than $100 million."[44] Yet, that is exactly what the provisions of ESA required.[45]

Moreover, a BO from the U.S. Fish and Wildlife Service (USFWS) finding that a federal activity will not adversely impact an endangered species is not necessarily the final word as to whether the federal activity can proceed. In *Center for Biological Diversity v. Rumsfeld*,[46] an Arizona federal court held that the U.S. Army and the Service were arbitrary and capricious in determining that activities at Fort Huachuca, Arizona, would not cause jeopardy to a rare plant, the Huachuca water umbel, or a rare bird, the Southwestern willow flycatcher. The decision concerned the Army's efforts to come up with a plan to mitigate the effects of groundwater pumping attributable to the Army's activities. "The whole premise of the 'no jeopardy' ruling," the district court judge wrote, "which is that within three years the Army and other interested parties will come up with a long-term plan to remedy the groundwater deficit problem, is an admission that what is currently on the table as far as mitigation measures is inadequate to support the FWS's 'no jeopardy' decision."[47]

Wetlands Protection

Wetlands compliance[48] should occur in concert with the NEPA process. Compliance generally requires the agency proponent to coordinate with the U.S. Army Corps of Engineers or to request special permits. Wetlands compliance is a controversial and difficult area of environmental law. At first glance, the law in this area may appear to be straightforward. In reality, the law is not so simple.

A permit from the U.S. Army Corps of Engineers (or a state with permitting authority) is required under Section 404 of the Clean Water Act for all discharges of dredged or fill material into "waters of the United States."[49] "Waters of the United States" include wetlands that are adjacent to or tributary to other waters of the United States.[50] Courts have even found nonadjacent wetlands to be waters of the United States based on their use by migratory waterfowl or interstate travelers, which constitutes a nexus to interstate commerce sufficient to establish federal jurisdiction.[51] The Supreme Court, however, overruled the "Migratory Bird Rule" in its 2001 decision, *Solid Waste Agency of Northern Cook County v. United States Army Corps of Engineers.*[52]

"Wetlands" are areas that are inundated or saturated by surface water or groundwater at a frequency and duration sufficient to support, and normally do support, vegetation that is typically adapted for life in saturated soil conditions, including swamps, marshes, bogs, and similar areas.[53] An area need not be saturated all year long to constitute a wetland.[54] Further, the concept of discharge or dredged or fill material can be interpreted extremely broadly. Proposed activities that affect a small creek bed or western arroyo, for instance, could require a Section 404 permit. The dredging or filling of a wetland, however, is not the only wetland activity that requires a permit.[55] The incidental discharge into a wetland by bulldozers or military vehicles—tracked vehicles, for instance—could trigger the requirement for a Section 404 permit. In those circumstances, the federal agency will normally consult with the Corps of Engineers to determine whether a Section 404 permit is required.[56] Such consultation may even be required in desert environments. In addition, with regard to any federal construction project that might damage wetlands, Executive Order 11990 requires the proponent agency to make a determination that "there is no practicable alternative" to the project and that the project includes "all practicable measures to minimize harm to wetlands."[57]

Cultural Resources Requirements

Another responsibility federal agencies must assume in environmental planning comes from Section 106 of the National Historic Preservation Act (NHPA).[58] Under Section 106, any federal "undertaking"[59] triggers a requirement to consult with the federal government's Advisory Council on Historic Preservation (ACHP) regarding the fate of districts, sites, buildings, structures, and objects that are eligible for the National Register of Historic Places.[60] These areas include archeological sites as well as historic structures.[61] Ordinarily, properties that are newer than fifty years old will not be considered to be eligible for the National Register.[62]

Under the ACHP's regulations, when a federal agency determines that a proposed action falls within the NHPA definition of an undertaking, the agency must consult with the state historic preservation officer (SHPO).[63] The agency must also solicit the views of public and private organizations, Native Americans, local governments, and other groups that are likely to have knowledge of or concerns with the Historic Register eligible properties.[64] The agency may proceed with the proposed project or action if the agency determines that the project or action will have "no effect" on Historic Register eligible properties,[65] the SHPO agrees with that determination, and there are no objections raised within fifteen days.[66] If the agency determines that there is an effect but that it is not adverse and the SHPO agrees, the agency may make a "no adverse effect" determination and advise the ACHP.

If there will be an adverse effect on historic properties, however, the agency must notify the ACHP and enter negotiations with the SHPO on a memorandum of agreement (MOA) to avoid or to mitigate the adverse effect.[67] The ACHP may enter this consultation process with or without a request from either the agency or the SHPO.[68] If the agency and the SHPO (and sometimes the ACHP) cannot reach an agreement, only the head of the federal agency (for example, the commissioner of the Bureau of Reclamation) may overrule the SHPO and the ACHP. The agency head may not delegate this responsibility.[69]

Federal agencies must follow Section 106 requirements when they directly undertake federal activities and when they are involved indirectly through funding, approving, permitting, or licensing.[70] In its regulations, the ACHP includes in its definition of a federal undertaking "any project, activity, or program that can result in changes in the character or use of historic properties, if any such historic properties are located in the area of potential effects."[71] Courts have interpreted "undertaking" to include a wide variety of actions, including military operations,[72] building leases,[73] land exchange agreements,[74] and revision of agency regulations.[75]

In addition to the NHPA, the Native American Graves Protection and Repatriation Act (NAGPRA)[76] and the Archaeological Resources Protection Act (ARPA)[77] can play important roles in the federal environmental planning process. NAGPRA requires that all federal agencies (and museums) that possess "Native American human remains and associated funerary objects"[78] compile an inventory and notify tribes that might have a cultural link to the remains and associated objects.[79] If the tribe desires, the agency must return the remains and associated objects to the tribe.[80] The agency must also provide a summary listing of "unassociated funerary objects, sacred objects, and cultural patrimony."[81] Because newly discovered remains or tribal objects would fall under the possession and control of the federal agency that discovers them, the federal agency would be required to provide similar notification to the tribes and give the tribes an opportunity for consultation and repatriation. Environmental planning in areas with a widespread historic presence of Native Americans must consider the potential effects of discovering Native American remains or tribal objects. Failure to comply with these requirements can cause problems with Native American tribes.

ARPA provides requirements for the protection of archeological sites. If archeological resources[82] are discovered during the course of a federal activity, and if they must be excavated, the proponent must seek approval for the excavation from the federal land manager.[83] Unauthorized excavation is prohibited under ARPA.[84] In addition, the incidental discovery of an archeological site will trigger the requirements of Section 106 of the NHPA.

Air Conformity Determinations

Section 176(c) of the Clean Air Act (CAA),[85] which was adopted with the 1990 amendments to the CAA, requires that all federal actions conform to any applicable state implementation plan (SIP).[86] Thus, federal facilities that are located in air pollution nonattainment[87] and maintenance areas[88] must ensure that any proposed action will conform to the SIP. Under the EPA's implementing regulations, a federal action means "any activity engaged in by a department, agency, or instrumentality of the Federal government, or any activity that a department, agency, or instrumentality of the Federal government supports in any way, provides financial assistance for, licenses, permits, or approves."[89]

The air conformity rule sets standards for maximum emissions limits allowed for various air pollutants in nonattainment and maintenance areas.[90] For actions that exceed those limits, the proponent federal agency must show that the action conforms to the SIP.[91] The federal agency can demonstrate conformity by indicating that the action is already accounted for in the SIP, that the emissions are offset by emission reductions elsewhere within the nonattainment or maintenance area, or that the action does not contribute to or increase the frequency of air standards violations.[92]

When making its conformity determination, a federal agency "must consider comments from any interested parties."[93] The EPA regulations require a thirty-day notice and comment period.[94] The proponent federal agency must also notify the EPA regional offices and state and local air quality agencies of the project or action.[95] The conformity analysis will normally be done in conjunction with the NEPA process because it is required prior to taking any action and because it has a public notice requirement similar to NEPA's requirement. In its comments to the air conformity rule, the EPA noted that "federal agencies should consider meeting the conformity public participation requirements at the same time as the NEPA requirements."[96] This would allow the proponent agency to streamline the conformity determination process yet remain consistent with its requirements.

Western Water Rights

For federal agencies that operate in the western United States, special rules regarding water rights also apply. The western states generally follow a legal regime known as the "Prior Appropriation Doctrine" in determining who is entitled to scarce water resources. The history of the doctrine is tied closely to the history of the West itself. The doctrine was derived from the principles of mining law, in which the first prospector to stake a claim is exclusively entitled to work that claim. The first case to recognize a right of prior appropriation was *Irwin v. Phillips*,[97] which settled a dispute over water rights between miners. As time passed, agricultural irrigation replaced mining as the primary use of water in the West, and the doctrine was applied to this new use as well. The basis of the Prior Appropriation Doctrine, like its mining law precursor, is "first in time, first in right."[98] In other words, the first person to take water from a stream and use it for a beneficial purpose becomes the "senior appropriator," and his or her water right to the amount of water diverted is superior to all other subsequent, or "junior," appropriators. Beneficial uses normally include domestic uses, irrigation, industrial uses, and general municipal uses. Sometimes they include aesthetic uses as well, such as swimming or boating.[99] Water rights are typically monitored intensely by local associations of appropriators, often known as ditch companies, by local water districts, and by state officials. The Prior Appropriation Doctrine, however, does not require that water rights be used either efficiently or wisely.[100]

Under the Prior Appropriation Doctrine, an appropriator can change the beneficial use of the water or transfer a water right to another party. An appropriator can change the point of diversion or the type of use, but only under conditions that would protect the rights of other appropriators.[101] Water rights might also be lost if they are not consistently and beneficially used. Failure to use a water right coupled with intent to abandon the right constitutes abandonment, leaving the right open for appropriation by another party.[102] In some states, statutes specify that nonuse for a specified period of time constitutes forfeiture.[103]

The Prior Appropriation Doctrine is not uniformly applied throughout the western states. Nine states have adopted a *pure* form of the doctrine, known as the "Colorado Doctrine."[104] Ten stats follow a hybrid water law system, which incorporates elements of riparian rights as well as prior appropriation.[105] While federal facilities enjoy some distinct advantages over private users in the western states, federal attorneys and engineers must be keenly aware of water rights systems in their respective states.

The biggest advantage federal agencies enjoy derives from the Supreme Court's 1908 decision *Winters v. United States.*[106] The *Winters* Court held that, although no mention of water rights was made at the time lands were reserved for two Montana Indian tribes, the reservation by the federal government of the land for the tribes constituted an implied reservation of water rights to support the tribes' agricultural pursuits, which was the purpose of the creation of the reservation.[107]

The *Winters* Doctrine was expanded in *Cappaert v. United States,*[108] which held that the United States was entitled to instream flows of groundwater needed to support a species of wildlife at a national monument.[109] The Court stressed that, because the proclamation creating the park made specific reference to a rare and unusual species of fish living in Devil's Hole, an underground spring at Death Valley National Monument, protection of the species was implied as a purpose for the reservation of the land.[110] The Court held that the United States, in reserving public land for a specific purpose, was entitled to all previously unappropriated waters "necessary to accomplish the purposes for which the reservation was created."[111]

In *United States v. New Mexico,*[112] however, the Supreme Court rejected the U.S. Forest Service's efforts to protect instream flows for aesthetic, recreational, and fish-preservation purposes in the Gila National Forest in New Mexico. In *New Mexico,* the majority of the Court based its decision on the notion that protection of instream flows for aesthetic purposes was outside the "relatively narrow purposes for which national forests were to be reserved."[113] Justice Lewis Powell questioned in dissent whether "the forests which Congress intended to 'improve and protect' are the still, silent, lifeless places envisioned by the Court. . . . The forests consist of the birds, animals, and fish—the wildlife—that inhabit them, as well as the trees, flowers, shrubs and grasses."[114]

The *New Mexico* decision is significant in that it illustrates the Court's reluctance to stretch the reserved water right beyond the purpose of the reservation of land. Federal agencies, therefore, that have responsibilities under ESA or other statutes, therefore, which were not a part of the initial reservation of land may have to work within the state appropriation system to acquire sufficient water rights to protect species. This sometimes puts federal agencies in a difficult position in attempting to balance its legal obligations under ESA and other environmental statutes with the demands of other water users.[115]

For challenges to a federal agency's water rights under state systems, however, the McCarran Amendment[116] provides only a limited waiver of sovereign immunity. The statute grants state jurisdiction over the United States in any "suit (1) for the adjudication of rights to the use of water of a river system or other source or (2) for the administration of such rights, where it appears that the United States is the owner of or is in the process of acquiring water rights by appropriation under state law, by purchase, by exchange, or otherwise, and the United States is a necessary party to such suit."[117] The statute, however, only applies to "general adjudications" involving all the water rights of all appropriators on a stream.[118] It does not waive sovereign immunity for challenges by individuals seeking to determine their relative priorities against the United States.[119]

A unique feature of the waiver of sovereign immunity under the McCarran Amendment is that it requires the federal government to defend itself in state courts when the required elements are met.[120] This differs from the process familiar to most federal attorneys, which calls for immediate removal to federal district court.[121] Thus, the McCarran Amendment sacrifices the "home field advantage" federal attorneys normally enjoy. The rationale behind allowing the state adjudication process to consider federal water rights within the states was the assumption that states were better equipped to deal with complex water rights questions. Not everyone agrees. "There is nothing about the reserved right," one critic wrote, "that cannot be fully and more simply resolved consistent with principles of federalism in a federal court declaratory judgment action, if the parties were willing to see it done that way."[122]

Environmental Planning Overseas

Each of the military services has maintained a substantial force outside the continental United States (known in military jargon as "CONUS"—meaning the continental United States but not including Alaska and Hawaii), and many of those troops are stationed in foreign countries. In the United States (including Alaska and Hawaii), NEPA is a clear requirement. Yet, it is not entirely clear what law applies in determining environmental impacts of U.S. forces overseas. Courts have generally held that NEPA does not apply outside the United States, except for Antarctica. Early decisions indicated that NEPA might apply abroad.[123] Subsequent decisions, however, solidified the notion that there would be no extraterritorial application of NEPA. The U.S. District Court for the District of Columbia, for instance, found in *NEPA Coalition of Japan v. Aspin* that Congress had not clearly expressed its intent to apply NEPA outside the United States, triggering the presumption against extraterritorial application.[124] In *Aspin*, plaintiffs were attempting to force DOD to prepare EISs for military facilities in Japan despite the fact that those operations were governed by long-standing treaty arrangements.

In 1979, President Carter signed Executive Order 12,114, which adopted the position that NEPA does not apply to U.S. government activities overseas but nevertheless establishes requirements that agencies consider the effect of their actions on the environment overseas in certain circumstances.[125] The executive order was based entirely on the president's independent authority over the administration of the executive branch and has no statutory underpinning. Unlike NEPA, its violation does not give rise to a cause of action to challenge a government decision in court by the public or any interested party.

The DOD directive implementing the executive order requires that proposed actions affecting the "global commons"—areas outside the jurisdiction of any nation—be subject to a documented decision process.[126] "The focus [with regard to the global commons]," the directive states, "is not the place of the action, but the location of the environment with respect to which there is significant harm."[127] The requirements apply to "major Federal actions that do significant harm" to the environment, and the documents required include "Environmental Assessments and Environmental Impact Statements," similar to NEPA.[128]

The DOD directive also requires environmental analysis for actions conducted in foreign countries or that affect a "protected global resource." No action is required "with respect to Federal actions that affect only the environment of a participating or otherwise involved foreign nation and that do not involve providing products or physical projects producing principal products, emissions, or effluents that are prohibited or strictly regulated by Federal law in the United States, or resources of global importance that have been designated for protection."[129] "Environmental Studies" conducted under the directive either bilaterally or multilaterally are required to contain a review of the affected environment, any significant actions taken to avoid or mitigate environmental harms, and a description of any other significant environmental issues as appropriate.[130] "Environmental Reviews" are documents that are prepared unilaterally by the United States and must include a description of the affected environment, predicted effect of the proposed action on the environment, and analysis of significant actions being taken to protect or improve the environment in light of the proposed action.[131] Exemptions to the requirement include actions that are not anticipated to cause significant environmental harm outside the United States, disaster and emergency relief efforts, actions taken by the president, or actions taken by or at the behest of the president or a cabinet officer in the course of armed conflict or when national security or national interest is involved.[132] Decisions as to whether an action is likely to cause significant harm to the environment "normally will be made in consultation with the concerned foreign governments or organizations."[133] If the military service determines that the action is not likely to cause significant environmental harm, then "the file will be documented with a record of that decision and the decision-makers who participated."[134]

If the agency proceeds with a study, however, then it can take no action with respect to the proposal that would harm the environment until the study is completed.[135] The contents of the study "must be flexible because of such considerations as the sensitivity of obtaining information from foreign governments, the availability of useful and understandable information, and other factors."[136] Still, each study "should" include a consideration of the affected environment, the predicted effects on the environment, actions taken by the governmental entities to "protect or improve" the environment, and, if no actions will be taken to "protect or enhance the environment, whether the decision not to do so was made by the affected foreign government or international organization."[137] Procedures "may be modified where necessary to . . . enable the component to act promptly; . . . avoid adverse impacts on relations between the United States and foreign governments; . . . avoid infringement or the appearance of infringement on the sovereign responsibilities of another government"; or to protect national security interests or governmental confidentiality.[138]

Along with NEPA, extraterritorial application of the Endangered Species Act is questionable. *Lujan v. Defenders of Wildlife* highlighted the difficulty of pursuing a case based on overseas impacts to endangered species.[139] In *Lujan*, the plaintiffs had sought to compel the U.S. Fish and Wildlife Service (USFWS) and the National Marine Fisheries Service (NMFS) to require consultation under ESA Section 7(a)(2) for actions taken by U.S. government agencies in foreign nations.[140] Although the USFWS and the NMFS had in 1978 issued a joint regulation stating that obligations imposed by Section 7(a)(2) extended to actions taken in foreign countries, the agencies reconsidered that position and in 1983 issued a revised joint regulation requiring consultation only for actions taken in the United States or on the high seas.[141]

At issue before the Supreme Court in *Lujan* was not the USFWS and NMFS regulation itself but the standing to challenge it. The *Lujan* plaintiffs, attempted to show standing by submitting affidavits by its members. In one affidavit, a member attested that she had traveled to Egypt and "observed the traditional habitat of the endangered nile crocodile there" and that she would suffer harm if she were unable to return to observe the habitat and the crocodile directly due to the United States' "role . . . in overseeing the rehabilitation of the Aswan High Dam . . . and developing . . . Egypt's . . . Master Water Plan." Another affidavit stated that another member had "observed the habitat" of other endangered species in Sri Lanka, which might be affected by a project of the Agency for International Development.[142] The Supreme Court, however, found that the affidavits did not support a finding of "actual or imminent" injury required to establish standing to challenge the ESA regulation.[143] In addition, the Court found that they failed to demonstrate redressability because they had not challenged "separate decisions to fund particular projects allegedly causing them harm" but rather a "more generalized level of Government action (rules regarding consultation), the invalidation of which would affect all overseas projects."[144]

After *Lujan*, it became difficult to imagine how any environmental organization could ever challenge the basic premise of the USFWS and the NMFS regarding the overseas applicability of ESA. *Lujan* left Executive Order 12,114 and its derivative DOD directive as the only legal authorities governing environmental analysis of the military's peacetime activities overseas. With its many broad exemptions, it would appear that overseas commanders have little to be concerned about as compared to comparable environmental planning requirements within the United States. Some would argue that environmental planning requirements even within the United States should offer a similar flexibility—that the requirements should act as a guide in planning government actions rather than as an expensive document-drafting exercise necessary only to avoid getting sued. The drawback of the overseas requirements are that they lack clear standards to ensure that minimum environmental protections are put into place, and there is no enforcement authority outside of the Department of Defense and the military services themselves.

Notes

1. 42 U.S.C. § 4332(2)(C).
2. 40 C.F.R. pts. 1500–1508 (1998).
3. See, e.g., 67 Fed. Reg. 15290, 32 C.F.R. pt. 651 (Mar. 29, 2002) (Final Rule, U.S. Department of Army, Reg. 200-2, Environmental Effects of Army Actions).
4. See 40 C.F.R. § 1508.9.
5. See, e.g., 32 C.F.R. § 651.32.
6. See, e.g., 32 C.F.R. § 651.35.
7. 40 C.F.R. § 1501.3.
8. 42 U.S.C. § 4332(2)(C).
9. 40 C.F.R. § 1500.4.
10. 40 C.F.R. § 1501.3.
11. 40 C.F.R. § 1501.4(c).
12. Such a decision, however, would likely be made only by policy-level officials in the agency.
13. 40 C.F.R. § 1501.3.

14. Culvert Cliffs' Coordinating Committee, Inc. v. U.S. Atomic Energy Commission, 449 F.2d 1109 (D.C. Cir. 1971).

15. Strycker's Bay Neighborhood Council v. Karlen, 444 U.S. 223 (1980).

16. Hanly v. Mitchell, 460 F.2d 640 (2d Cir. 1972).

17. Hanly v. Kleindienst, 471 F.2d 823, 830–31 (2d Cir. 1972).

18. 40 C.F.R. § 1502.14(d).

19. Exec. Order No. 12, 898, 59 Fed. Reg. 7629 (1994).

20. 40 C.F.R. § 1501.2.

21. 40 C.F.R. § 1506.1.

22. Town of Huntington v. Marsh, 859 F.2d 1134 (2d Cir. 1988).

23. 40 C.F.R. § 1502.20.

24. *Id.*

25. 40 C.F.R. § 1502.21.

26. Robertson v. Methow Valley Citizens Council, 490 U.S. 332 (1989).

27. Town of Huntington v. Marsh, 859 F.2d 1134 (2d Cir. 1988).

28. United States v. Students Challenging Regulatory Agency Procedures, 412 U.S. 289 (1973).

29. 40 C.F.R. § 1506.11.

30. *Id.*

31. Valley Citizens for a Safe Environment v. Aldridge, 969 F.2d 1315 (1st Cir. 1992).

32. 16 U.S.C. §§ 1531–34.

33. Federal agencies consult with the U.S. Fish and Wildlife Service regarding land-based species and habitat or the Marine and Fisheries Service regarding ocean-based species and habitat.

34. 16 U.S.C. § 1536.

35. "Major construction" is a "construction project or similar activity on a scale that would trigger the requirement for an Environmental Impact Statement by significantly affecting the quality of the human environment." 50 C.F.R. § 402.02.

36. A "biological assessment" is "information prepared by or under the direction of the Federal agency concerning listed and proposed species and designated and proposed critical habitat that may be present in the action area and the evaluation of potential effects of the action on such species and habitat." 50 C.F.R. § 402.02.

37. 16 U.S.C. § 1536. A "biological opinion" states the opinion of the U.S. Fish and Wildlife Service "as to whether or not the Federal action is likely to jeopardize the continued existence of listed species or result in the destruction or adverse modification of critical habitat." 50 C.F.R. § 402.02.

38. This refers to damage to a species or its critical habitat "that result[s] from, but [is] not the purpose of, carrying out an otherwise lawful activity conducted by the Federal agency or applicant." 50 C.F.R. § 402.02. "Take" means to "harass, harm, pursue, hunt, shoot, wound, kill, trap, capture, or collect, or to attempt to engage in any such conduct." 16 U.S.C. § 1532(20).

39. 16 U.S.C. § 1536.

40. 16 U.S.C. § 1536(b)(4).

41. 16 U.S.C. § 1536(a)(2).

42. 16 U.S.C. § 1536(h).

43. Tennessee Valley Authority v. Hill, 437 U.S. 153 (1978).

44. *Id.* at 172–73.

45. *Id.*

46. Center for Biological Diversity v. Rumsfeld, No. 99-203 (D. Ariz. 2002).

47. *Id.* at 17.

48. 33 U.S.C. § 1344.

49. *Id.*

50. See, e.g., United States v. Riverside Bayview Homes, Inc., 474 U.S. 121 (1985).

51. See, e.g., Leslie Salt Co. v. Froehlke, 578 F.2d 742 (9th Cir. 1978). But see Tabb Lakes Ltd. v. United States, 10 F.2d 796 (Fed. Cir. 1993) (viewing this approach with disfavor).

52. Solid Waste Agency of Northern Cook County v. United States Army Corps of Engineers, 531 U.S. 159 (2001). For further deliberations on the extent of jurisdictional wetlands, see *Rapanos v. United States*, 126 S.Ct. 2208 (2006).

53. 40 C.F.R. § 122.2.

54. *Id.*

55. 33 U.S.C. § 1344.

56. *Id.*

57. Exec. Order No. 11, 990, 42 Fed. Reg. 26,961 (1977).

58. 16 U.S.C. § 470f. In addition to Section 106, Section 110 of the NHPA requires that federal agencies use their historic properties "to the maximum extent possible" rather than acquire or construct new properties (§ 470h-2). Section 110 also requires that federal agencies locate agency-owned historic properties and nominate those properties to the National Register of Historic Places.

59. "Undertaking" includes "any project, activity, or program that can result in changes in the character or use of historic properties, if any such historic properties are located in the area of potential effects. . . . Undertakings include new and continuing projects, activities, or programs and any of their elements not previously considered under Section 106." 16 U.S.C. § 470w(7).

60. 16 U.S.C. § 470f.

61. For instance, archeologists at the U.S. Army's Fort Bliss, Texas, estimate that the installation has more than 15,000 archeological sites within its boundaries. Interview with James Bowman, chief archeologist, Fort Bliss, Tex. (Nov. 12, 1997).

62. 36 C.F.R. § 60.4.

63. 36 C.F.R. § 800.4(a).

64. 36 C.F.R. § 800.2(e).

65. This provision also applies to projects that will have no effect on the "area of potential effects," which is defined as the geographic area or areas within which the undertaking may cause changes in the character or use of historic properties. *Id.* § 800.2(c).

66. 36 C.F.R. § 800.5(b).

67. 36 C.F.R. § 800.5(e).

68. *Id.*

69. 16 U.S.C. § 470h.

70. 16 U.S.C. § 470w(7).

71. 36 C.F.R. § 800.2(o).

72. Barcelo v. Brown, 478 F. Supp. 646 (D.P.R. 1979).

73. Birmingham Realty Co. v. General Serv. Admin., 497 F. Supp. 1377 (N.D. Ala. 1980).

74. Daingerfield Island Protective Society v. Babbitt, 40 F.3d 442 (D.C. Cir. 1994).

75. Illinois Interstate Commerce Commission v. Interstate Commerce Commission, 848 F.2d 1246 (D.C. Cir. 1988).

76. 25 U.S.C. §§ 3001–13.

77. 16 U.S.C. §§ 470aa–470ll.

78. "Native American" means of or related to a "tribe, people, or culture that is indigenous to the United States." 25 U.S.C. § 3001(9). "Associated funerary objects" means objects that were a part of the "death rite or ceremony of a culture" and were placed with the body at the time of burial or later (§ 3001[3][A]).

79. 25 U.S.C. § 3003.

80. 25 U.S.C. § 3005.

81. "Unassociated funerary objects" include objects that are not presently under the control of the federal agency. 25 U.S.C. § 3001(3)(B). "Sacred objects" are specific ceremonial objects for the practice of Native American religions (§ 3001[3][C]). "Cultural patrimony" includes objects that have cultural significance to an entire tribe, rather than to an individual member of the tribe (§ 3001[3][D]).

82. "Archeological resource [means] any material remains of past human life or activities which are of archeological interest . . . [including] pottery, basketry, bottles, weapons, weapon projectiles, tools, structures, or portions of structures, pit houses, rock paintings, rock carvings, intaglios, graves, human skeletal remains, or any portion or piece of any of the foregoing items." 16 U.S.C. § 470bb(1).

83. 16 U.S.C. § 470cc. "Federal land manager" means the secretary of the department "having primary management authority over such lands."

84. 16 U.S.C. § 470ee. In addition, information about the sites must be kept confidential (§ 470hh).

85. 42 U.S.C. § 7506(c).

86. *Id.* A "SIP" is a state's source-specific plan for meeting air quality standards.

87. "Nonattainment areas" are areas that do not meet national air quality standards for a particular pollutant. 40 C.F.R. pt. 50.

88. A "maintenance area" is an area that meets air quality standards but must have a plan to keep its emissions in compliance. 40 C.F.R. § 51.852.

89. *Id.*

90. 40 C.F.R. § 853(b)(1).

91. 40 C.F.R. § 51.

92. 40 C.F.R. § 51.858.

93. 40 C.F.R. § 51.854.

94. 40 C.F.R. § 51.856(b).

95. 40 C.F.R. § 51.855(a).

96. 58 Fed. Reg. 63,214 (1993).

97. Irwin v. Phillips, 5 Calif. 140 (1855).

98. David Getches, Water Law in a Nutshell 141–43 (1984).

99. KENNETH R. WRIGHT, ED., WATER RIGHTS OF THE FIFTY STATES AND TERRITORIES 26 (1990).

100. This has been the subject of criticism among those who argue that the Prior Appropriation Doctrine is obsolete. See, e.g., Charles F. Wilkinson, *Aldo Leopold and Western Water Law: Thinking Perpendicular to the Prior Appropriation Doctrine*, 14 LAND & WATER L. REV. 1 (1989).

101. WRIGHT, WATER RIGHTS at 27–28.

102. *Id.* at 28.

103. *Id.*

104. Coffin v. Left Hand Ditch Co., 6 Colo. 443 (1882). In addition to Colorado, the states of New Mexico, Wyoming, Montana, Idaho, Utah, Nevada, Arizona, and Alaska follow the "Colorado Doctrine."

105. The hybrid states are Texas, Kansas, Nebraska, North Dakota, South Dakota, Oklahoma, Washington, California, Oregon, and Mississippi.

106. Winters v. United States, 207 U.S. 564 (1908).

107. *Id.* at 576–77.

108. Cappaert v. United States, 426 U.S. 128 (1976).

109. *Id.* at 132.

110. *Id.*

111. *Id.* at 139.

112. United States v. New Mexico, 438 U.S. 696 (1978).

113. *Id.* at 709. The Court held that national forests were reserved for two primary purposes: timber preservation and enhancement of water supply.

114. *Id.* at 719.

115. See William A. Wilcox Jr., *Western Flood Management in the 21st Century: A Tightrope between Competing Values*, W. WATER L. & POL. REP. 153 (Apr. 2000).

116. 43 U.S.C. § 666.

117. *Id.*

118. Dugan v. Rank, 372 U.S. 609, 618 (1963).

119. See Michael D. White, *McCarran Amendment Adjudications—Problems, Solution, Alternative*, 22 LAND & WATER L. REV. 619 (1987).

120. 43 U.S.C. § 666.

121. 28 U.S.C. § 2679.

122. Joseph Membrino, *Indian Reserved Water Rights, Federalism, and the Trust Responsibility*, 27 LAND & WATER L. REV. 1, 4 (1992).

123. See, e.g., *Sierra Club v. Adams*, 578 F.2d 389 (D.C. Cir. 1978).

124. *NEPA Coalition of Japan v. Aspin*, 837 F. Supp. 466 (D. D.C. 1993).

125. Exec. Order No. 12,114, 44 Fed. Reg. 1957 (1979).

126. ENVIRONMENTAL EFFECTS ABROAD OF MAJOR DEPARTMENT OF DEFENSE ACTIONS, Department of Defense Directive 6050.7, Enclosure 1, E1.3, Mar. 31, 1979.

127. *Id.* at Enclosure 1, E1.1.

128. *Id.* at Enclosure 1, E1.3.9, E1.4.

129. *Id.* at Enclosure 2, E2.2.2.

130. *Id.* at Enclosure 2, E2.4.

131. *Id.* at Enclosure 2, E2.5.

132. *Id.* at Enclosure 2, E2.3.3.
133. *Id.* at Enclosure 2, E2.4.3.
134. *Id.*
135. *Id.*
136. *Id.* at Enclosure 2, E2.4.4.
137. *Id.*
138. *Id.* at Enclosure 2, E2.4.6.
139. Lujan v. Defenders of Wildlife, 504 U.S. 555 (1992).
140. Id. at 558–59.
141. *Id.*
142. *Id.* at 563.
143. *Id.* at 564.
144. *Id.* at 568.

4

Emerging Issues concerning Military Operations

THE REGULATORY AND COMPLIANCE POSTURE of the military is constantly changing. New issues are emerging, driven by changing circumstances and views. The balance between environmental protection and accomplishing effective training for war frequently presents novel issues. Among the prominent issues unique to the military today are determining how military munitions should be treated within the environmental law framework, determining when to apply national security exemptions in environmental law, and protecting military training on land and at sea from being compromised by environmental "encroachment" issues.

Military Munitions

Military munitions are inherent to the military mission, and they pose special problems for both environmental regulators and the military services. With changes in military threats and expectations, both in size and structure, since the close of the Cold War, the military must deal with vast stockpiles of unused munitions throughout the country. In addition, the military no longer has the need for many of the training ranges that were active for decades from World Wars I and II through the Cold War. Most of those ranges are littered with spent munitions and unexploded ordnance. Although much of these munitions materials would be considered "reactive" within the meaning of the Resource Conservation and Recovery Act (RCRA), the point at which munitions become a "waste" was an open question. RCRA defines the term "solid waste" to include "garbage, refuse, sludge from a waste treatment plant, water supply treatment plant, or air pollution control facility and other discarded material, including solid, liquid, semisolid, or contained gaseous material resulting from industrial, commercial, mining, and agricultural operations, and from community activities."[1] In the military's traditional view, when firing a round downrange, an artilleryman wasn't "discarding" the round. Rather, he was using the material for the purpose intended, even though he had no intention of retrieving it and using it again. Since the fired round was not a waste, it was not regulated under RCRA; rather, the military tended to view military munitions, including unexploded ordnance, as safety hazards rather than environmental cleanup imperatives. State regulators tended to view the round, once it landed on the range, as a de facto discarded item. In adopting the Federal Facilities Compliance Act (FFCA) in 1992, Congress made an attempt to provide a solution to this impasse. It directed the Environmental Protection Agency (EPA) to consider special regulations for military munitions and called for consultation between the EPA and the Department of Defense (DOD) to determine when military munitions would become subject to RCRA's regulatory scheme.[2]

After extensive discussion between the government departments, the resulting product was the Military Munitions Rule (MMR).[3] The MMR became effective on August 12, 1997. Military munitions wastes are defined as "solid wastes" within the MMR.[4] That definition, however, does not mean that munitions wastes are not hazardous wastes. They may still be regulated as hazardous wastes if they exhibit one of the characteristics associated with hazardous wastes, such as reactivity.[5] Under the MMR, an unused munition is not a waste until it has been abandoned by being disposed of, burned, or treated prior to disposal;[6] removed from storage for the purpose of being disposed of;[7] damaged to the point that it cannot be repaired and cannot be recycled or used for another purpose;[8] or has been determined to be a solid waste by an authorized military official.[9] Munitions on active ranges and inactive ranges that are potentially active are not considered a solid waste as long as they are used for their intended purpose, which includes munitions that are used for the training of military personnel and of explosives and emergency response specialists;[10] munitions that are used for research, development, testing, and evaluation;[11] and munitions that are destroyed during certain range clearance operations.[12] When munitions on active ranges are handled for disposal, they become a solid waste unless they are destroyed in emergency response actions. The MMR does not apply to closed ranges, and regulators may still have to wrangle with the military regarding when a spent munition becomes a waste at closed ranges.

The EPA encourages states to adopt the terms and provisions of the MMR; however, it acknowledges that states may adopt requirements with respect to military munitions that are more stringent or broader in scope than the federal requirements. Only a handful of states authorized to administer their own hazardous waste programs have yet to adopt the MMR.[13]

The MMR, to the degree it has been adopted by states, provides a measure of certainty respecting the regulatory status of military munitions that fall within the rule. Without that certainty, munitions left on closed ranges are subject to a range of interpretations—from being considered "discarded material" under 42 U.S.C. Section 6903 and thus possibly subject to the Comprehensive Environmental Response, Compensation, and Liability Act (CERCLA) or RCRA corrective action requirements to being considered, in the DOD's view, material used for the purpose intended and thus not a waste at all. The DOD attempted to close the gap in authorities with a draft "Range Rule," which would have applied to closed, transferred, and transferring (CTT) ranges and was published in the Federal Register in 1997 but, because of resistance from the environmental community, never finalized.[14] The DOD in the year 2000 opted instead to enter into a bilateral memorandum of understanding with the EPA on "Unexploded Ordnance (UXO) Management Principles."[15] Because it was never adopted as a final regulation, this memorandum cannot be considered to have the force of law. However, because its principal signatories were the DOD and the EPA, it is instructive. In it, the DOD reiterated its commitment to adopting the "Range Rule" and agreed to conduct response actions for explosives safety hazards, including UXO, following a CERCLA-like process "to address human health, environmental, and explosives safety concerns on CTT ranges."[16] State authority to regulate on CTT ranges is ambiguous. If a property is subject to a RCRA facility permit, a state may have a sharp regulatory hook on which to base RCRA corrective action requirements. A state may also attempt to exert authority under "mini-CERCLA" environmental cleanup laws,[17] but if the property remains in the ownership of the federal government, such an argument would likely be contested on the ground that, although the federal government must follow state substantive requirements, the federal government has not waived sovereign immunity for state regulatory enforcement authority under CERCLA.[18]

In addition, under the recently promulgated Munitions Response Site Prioritization Protocol (MRSPP),[19] the DOD adopted standards for prioritizing munitions cleanup sites on DOD-owned, leased, or controlled property in the United States, excluding operational ranges, treatment facilities, and manufacturing and storage facilities. The rule was promulgated in response to Congress's mandate in the National Defense Authorization Act for Fiscal Year 2002, which required the DOD to develop an initial inventory of sites known or suspected to contain military munitions and a comprehensive plan for cleanup. The rule requires the DOD to seek regulator and community involvement in the prioritization process.[20] In sequencing response activities, the DOD components must consider such factors as concerns expressed by regulators and other stakeholders, cultural and social factors, economic factors, ecological risk factors, anticipated reuse, and mission-driven requirements.[21]

Still, issues involved with military munitions responses have consistently vexed the military services. In December 2003, the General Accounting Office (GAO—now known as the Government Accountability Office) completed a study of the DOD's munitions response program, concluding that the DOD "does not yet have a complete and viable plan for cleaning up military munitions at remaining potentially contaminated sites."[22] The GAO report found that the Pentagon had made only "limited progress" on cleaning up some 15 million acres of property that are known or suspected to be contaminated with military munitions.[23] The report recommended that the services establish stricter deadlines for identifying and evaluating sites, reassess the timetable proposed for reevaluating sites using new risk assessment procedures, and establish interim goals for cleanup phases.[24]

Another recent emerging issue with respect to munitions concerns perchlorate, a previously unregulated substance that is a primary ingredient of solid rocket propellant. The most common variety is ammonium. The regulatory status of perchlorate is a developing issue in the United States. Although there is concern that perchlorate may pose health risks at certain levels of exposure, the military services believe neither the EPA nor the states have complete scientific data to establish comprehensive cleanup standards. The EPA has established an official reference dose (RfD) of 0.0007 mg/kg/day of perchlorate. According to the EPA, this level is consistent with the National Academy of Science's recommended reference dose. A reference dose is a scientific estimate of a daily exposure level that is not expected to cause adverse health effects in humans. While occurring most frequently at domestic Air Force installations, ammonium perchlorate has been detected at Army and Navy sites, too. Perchlorate contamination is an issue at both active and closed installations.[25]

National Security Exemptions

The environmental regulatory statutes generally provide a means for the president to exempt a military service from compliance when it is imperative to the national defense, although such exemptions are rarely used. Under the Clean Water Act, for instance, the president may exempt from compliance any "weaponry, equipment, aircraft, vessels, vehicles, or other classes or categories of property."[26] Professor Stephen Dycus used the controversy over the Navy's unpermitted firing into the Pacific Ocean at Vieques Island, Puerto Rico, to demonstrate the preference for compliance, even if belated, over noncompliance. In the resulting court battle, the Supreme Court ultimately rejected Puerto Rico's argument that the Navy's remedy was to seek a presidential exemption, noting that ordering the Navy to apply for a permit but refusing to grant an injunction came closer to meeting the purpose of the statute, which was to encourage compliance.[27]

Similarly, the Clean Air Act (CAA) allows an exemption for a federal emission source if the president determines it to be in the "paramount interest of the United States." He may also extend the exemption to "weaponry, equipment, aircraft, vehicles, or other classes or categories of property which are owned or operated by the Armed Forces."[28] The CAA exemption was invoked by President James Earl Carter in 1980 in a situation involving the relocation of approximately 114,000 Haitian and Cuban "Boat Lift" refugees to Fort Allen, Puerto Rico, a naval communications center. In response to local objections that the relocation to Fort Allen violated environmental laws, the president signed Executive Order 12,244, which exempted Fort Allen emissions sources "from compliance with the provisions of the [CAA]."[29] There is no such exemption for new sources, and an exemption from requirement for hazardous air pollutants is only available when no technology is available to comply.

RCRA also gives the president authority to exempt a federal agency from its requirements if it is in the "paramount interest of the United States to do so."[30] The exemption can last no longer than a year, with subsequent one-year exemptions granted only by a separate determination by the president for each period of exemption and an annual report to Congress giving the reason for each exemption.[31] A court challenge regarding the Air Force's operations at Groom Lake, Nevada, involved a RCRA presidential exemption. Following President Clinton's granting an exemption of operations "that would require the disclosure of classified information that operating location to any unauthorized person,"[32] the Ninth Circuit upheld the exemption against arguments that the president could exempt a facility from RCRA but not documents because of their status. The court held that it was in the president's discretion to determine what was in "the paramount interest of the United States."[33]

In spite of the potential for waivers from environmental laws for national security reasons, it has been argued that the rarely used exemptions are generally too narrow and contemplate limited, one-time uses. In a 2004 article in the *Air Force Law Review*, for instance, three Air Force colonels argued that the exemptions currently provided in environmental law are not enough. "Although DoD might be able to take greater advantage of these exemptions from time to time, the bottom line is that we must be able to train the way we fight, and we must be able to operate to defend the country in its interests," they wrote. "Individual pieces of this day-to-day training are difficult to quantify in absolute national security terms. . . . The aggregate result of having to employ these exemptions on a case-by-case basis might be 'death by a thousand cuts.' The death in question being the totality of realistic training for the military."[34] Unfortunately, lacking any evidence to demonstrate how lack of certain environmental law exemptions impedes training, the colonels' arguments don't support their conclusions. In fact, replete with examples of instances in which presidential exemptions have been invoked and upheld by the courts, the article tends to bolster the counterargument that existing exemptions should be sufficient to provide for military contingencies.

The Readiness and Range Preservation Initiative

Reflected in the three colonels' call for wider exemptions was a widespread frustration in the Department of Defense with environmental restrictions that at times seem to make no sense to military commanders. In 2002, following a GAO report that expressed concerns over civilian "encroachment" on military training[35] and with a sympathetic Republican majority in Congress, the Pentagon attempted to push back against those restrictions, announcing a "major effort to address encroachment, sustain our training and testing ranges, and maintain force readiness."[36] Encroachment, according to the 2002 GAO report, had included unplanned or incompatible commercial or residential development around installations, competition for airspace, competition for frequency spectrum, designation of critical habitat under the Endangered Species Act (ESA), and potential environmental regulation of military munitions, air quality issues, and noise.[37] The GAO report concluded that encroachment "has limited the extent to which training ranges are available or the types of training that can be conducted."[38] The GAO report also found, however, that the Pentagon had not produced sufficient data to show "to what extent encroachment has significantly affected training readiness or costs, even though officials in congressional testimonies and other forums cited examples of encroachment at times preventing the services from training as they would like to."[39]

Deputy Undersecretary of Defense Raymond Dubois, in explaining efforts to recast the balance between the environment and military training, explained that the Readiness and Range Preservation Initiative (RRPI) was not seeking exemptions from environmental law but rather "seeking to strike a sensible balance between these two national imperatives."[40] The RRPI effort sought statutory recognition within RCRA, the Endangered Species Act, and the CAA and other environmental statutes that actions typical of military operations did not violate environmental laws.[41]

As an example of environmental laws that impeded military training, DOD officials cited the Migratory Bird Treaty Act (MBTA),[42] which is a statute enacted in 1918 to implement the International Convention for the Protection of Migratory Birds.[43] In *Center for Biological Diversity v. Pirie*,[44] the District Court for the District of Columbia held that the Navy had violated the act by live fire training activities without a permit that sometimes killed migratory birds on an island in the Marianas and temporarily enjoined military training until the Navy sought a permit for the incidental "taking" (e.g., killing) of migratory birds. The MBTA became one of the first targets of the DOD's efforts to seek statutory relief from environmental laws in 2002.

DOD officials have stated that they have found ways to comply with environmentally restrictive laws but at a high cost. "While in some cases, based on the creative minds of military planners and their environmental teams, there are and have been feasible training workarounds, all too often, such workarounds chip away at the basic fabric and underpinnings of the training objectives," wrote Assistant Deputy Undersecretary Alex Beehler and Lt. Col. Ann Erin Mercer. "Where once a thousand troops could train together, now only a hundred can operate."[45]

As could be expected the legislative proposals drew immediate opposition. States attorneys general argued that there was no evidence that RCRA, CERCLA, or the CAA had adversely affected military readiness.[46] "As of this writing, DoD has still not identified a single example where any of these laws has actually caused an adverse impact on military readiness," the attorneys general wrote.[47] "Given the widespread contamination from military activities," the attorneys general continued, "and the responsible track record states have developed over the past two decades of regulating the environmental aspects of military activities, we do not think that 'uncertainties about future application and enforcement' of these environmental laws justifies preempting state and EPA authority over cleanup of munitions-related contamination at potentially thousands of sites around the country."[48]

Some critics saw the measure as a part of a larger effort by the George W. Bush administration to roll back environmental protections generally by chipping away, first, at laws few Americans sympathize with but over time creating a greater tolerance for changing all environmental laws.[49] Others joined the state attorneys general in questioning the need for legislative changes. "The Defense Department claims that environmental compliance has jeopardized military readiness," wrote Professor Dycus. "But there is almost no evidence to support that claim. . . . The military's stunning successes in Afghanistan and Iraq were achieved using troops trained and weapons tested under existing environmental statutes and regulations."[50]

Efforts to alter the applicability of certain environmental laws to military activities even caused some conflict within the Bush administration itself. Having listened to testimony before the Senate Armed Services Subcommittee on Readiness and Management Support, then-EPA Administrator Christine Todd Whitman wrote a letter to Defense Secretary Donald Rumsfeld explaining that she was surprised to hear testimony from DOD witnesses "creating the impression that EPA has prevented vital military training."[51] She recounted some of the testimony that was given during the hearings, explaining that she was only aware of one instance in which enforcement of EPA regulations had affected training—at Massachusetts Military Reservation in Cape Cod, where EPA took action "only after other efforts failed to stop the spread of contamination to the only source of drinking water for hundreds of thousands of people."[52]

Rumsfeld, however, wasn't moved. "The fact remains that the manner in which certain environmental laws are being applied is seriously hampering our military training opportunities in several areas of the United States," he stated in his brief reply. "It is a big problem and we are grateful for your assistance in helping us address the matter. I am certain we can protect the environment without unduly restricting our ability to train our armed forces."[53]

Although the Pentagon would continue to push its agenda, the RRPI legislation initially met with mixed results. Pentagon efforts to reshape environmental laws were more successful in the arena of wildlife laws than in reforming the major statutes regulating pollution. Congress in 2002 approved a measure allowing incidental taking of migratory birds by the military so long as they were a result of military readiness activities, an exemption intended to last until the U.S. Fish and Wildlife Service developed regulations for issuance of incidental take permits.[54] In related legislation the following term, Congress approved an amendment to the Endangered Species Act providing that the U.S. Fish and Wildlife Service would not designate any DOD-controlled lands that are subject to an Integrated Natural Resources Management Plan (INRMP).[55] Military facilities are required to prepare an INRMP under the Sikes Act.[56] Congress in 2003 also created a broad exemption in the Marine Mammal Protection Act[57] for "national defense," and redefined, with respect to the military activities, "harassment" of species to require greater scientific evidence of harm.[58] These measures incrementally diminish the legal protections of the species concerned. It remains to be seen how much they will result in actual harm to species populations. With responsible stewardship by military commanders, it is possible that harm to species will be negligible. If commanders attempt to aggressively exploit the relaxed requirements, however, damages to species could be significant.

Navy Sonar and Operations at Sea

Since the mid-1990s, environmentalists and the U.S. Navy have been at odds over the effects of sonar on marine mammals. Similar to ESA, the Marine Mammal Protection Act (MMPA)[59] provides protection against the "taking" of marine mammals in U.S. waters. The Navy's sonar creates a high intensity pulse of sound, often called a "ping," the resonance of which and the interpretation of received echoes can reveal the presence of undersea objects.[60] Transmission of sonar at certain frequencies has prompted concerns that the sonar could physically damage the hearing in cetaceans (i.e., dolphins, whales, and porpoises) or cause them to change their habits in ways that would be detrimental to their survival.[61] Midfrequency sonar has been implicated in several beaked whale strandings, but much about sonar's effects on marine mammals is yet unknown. However, sonar has been considered to be subject to the provisions of the MMPA, which prohibits taking the marine mammals without an incidental take permit (letter of authorization).[62] Impacts of noise on marine mammals have also been considered by the Navy to be an environmental impact appropriate for analysis under the National Environmental Policy Act (NEPA).[63]

In 1996, the Navy published a notice of intent to prepare an environmental impact statement (EIS) for the proposed use of the Surveillance Towed Array Sensor System (SURTASS), a form of low-frequency active (LFA) sonar.[64] In 1999, the Navy released its draft EIS on the SURTASS system and submitted an application to the National Marine Fisheries Service (NMFS) for a letter of authorization to harass marine mammals incidental to use of the SURTASS sonar and, later, sought formal consultation pursuant to Section 7 of ESA.[65] In 2001, the Navy released its final EIS for the SURTASS sonar system, and the NMFS published a proposed rule authorizing the Navy to harass marine mammals incidental to the use of the SURTASS system, but the independent Marine Mammal Commission commented that under the NMFS's proposed rule it was not clear that only negligible effects on marine mammals would result—a requirement for obtaining the letter of authorization.[66] But the NMFS's final rule permitting harassment of marine mammals became effective August 15, 2002.[67]

The Natural Resources Defense Council (NRDC) and other environmental groups sued, seeking a halt to deployment of the SURTASS sonar and attempting to compel the Navy to prepare a programmatic EIS on its Littoral Warfare Advanced Development program. With respect to the demand for a programmatic EIS, the federal district court determined that the program was not subject to a programmatic challenge under NEPA or ESA.[68] However, the environmental groups had more success with respect to their specific challenge to deployment of the SURTASS system, obtaining a preliminary injunction in California limiting deployment of the sonar.[69] The Navy and environmental groups soon entered a stipulated agreement allowing the Navy to conduct limited testing of the SURTASS LFA pending consideration of the federal lawsuit.[70] The court later determined that the NMFS's take authorization was improperly granted and ordered the parties to negotiate the terms of a permanent injunction that would allow the Navy to meet its needs by operating the SURTASS LFA in a limited way.[71] In a concurrent case, a federal judge granted a temporary injunction to block testing of a high-frequency civilian whale-finding sonar off the California coast, concluding that the NMFS's use of a categorical exclusion to support its decision was unjustified.[72]

After President Bush in 2003 signed the National Defense Authorization Act for Fiscal Year 2004, which included a provision that provided for a modification of the definition of "harassment" applicable to military activities under the MMPA, the Ninth Circuit held that marine mammals lacked standing to sue the government over sonar.[73] Meanwhile, the potential harm of sonar on whales gained international attention and prompted several international organizations, including the European Union, to call for limitations on the use of high-intensity sonar.[74] Despite the rising tide of opposition, however, the Navy continued plans to implement the SURTASS LFA, moving forward with plans in 2005 to create a sonar training range off North Carolina.[75]

On July 3, 2006, the NRDC and its environmental allies succeeded in securing a temporary restraining order against the deployment of midfrequency active (MFA) sonar during a training exercise, finding that the plaintiffs had submitted "considerable convincing scientific evidence demonstrating that the Navy's use of MFA sonar can kill, injure, and disturb many marine species, including marine mammals."[76] Days later, the Navy and the NRDC announced a settlement that would allow the Navy to operate during the exercise with safeguards, including a "sonar-free buffer zone" surrounding the Marine National Monument near Hawaii and monitoring for marine mammals during sonar drills.[77]

Notes

1. 42 U.S.C. § 6903(27).

2. Federal Facilities Compliance Act, Pub. L. No. 102-386 (1992), § 107, 106 Stat. 1513 (amending RCRA § 3004, 42 U.S.C. § 6924).

3. 40 C.F.R. § 266.200; Military Munitions Rule: Hazardous Waste Identification and Management; Explosives Emergencies; Manifest Exemption for Transport of Hazardous Waste on Right-of-Ways on Contiguous Properties, 62 Fed. Reg. 6622, 6628 (1997).

4. 40 C.F.R. § 261.2(a)(2)(iv).
5. 40 C.F.R. § 261.3(1).
6. 40 C.F.R. § 266.202(b)(1).
7. 40 C.F.R. § 266.202(b)(2).
8. 40 C.F.R. § 266.202(b)(3).
9. 40 C.F.R. § 266.202(b)(4).
10. 40 C.F.R. § 266.202(a)(1)(i).
11. 40 C.F.R. § 266.202(a)(1)(ii).
12. 40 C.F.R. § 266.202(a)(1)(iii).
13. The rule went into effect for non-RCRA authorized states Alaska, Hawaii, and Iowa on August 12, 1997. It was subsequently adopted by Alabama, Arkansas, Delaware, District of Columbia, Florida, Georgia, Idaho, Illinois, Indiana, Kansas, Louisiana, Mississippi, Missouri, Montana, Nevada, New Jersey, New Mexico, North Carolina, Oklahoma, Pennsylvania, Puerto Rico, South Carolina, South Dakota, Tennessee, Virginia, and West Virginia. Arizona, Colorado, and Nebraska adopted the rule with only minor modifications. Michigan, New York, Oregon, and Texas adopted significantly different variations of the MMR.
14. 62 Fed. Reg. 50796 (Sept. 26, 1997).
15. DOD and EPA Memorandum, subject: Unexploded Ordnance (UXO) Management Principles, Mar. 7, 2000.
16. *Id.* at 3.
17. See, e.g., Calif. Health & Safety Code § 25300 et seq.
18. See 42 U.S.C. § 9620(a)(2).
19. 70 Fed. Reg. 58016 (Oct. 5, 2005) (to be codified at 32 C.F.R. pt. 179).
20. *Id.* § 179.5(c).
21. *Id.* § 179.7(a).
22. General Accounting Office, Military Munitions: DoD Needs to Develop a Comprehensive Approach for Cleaning Up Contaminated Sites, report to the Honorable John D. Dingell, Ranking Minority Member, Committee on Energy and Commerce, House of Representatives, Dec. 19, 2003, at 18.
23. *Id.*
24. *Id.*
25. For a discussion of regulatory developments respecting perchlorate, see the EPA's website at www.epa.gov/fedfac/documents/perchlorate.htm (accessed Sept. 4, 2006). See also Interstate Technology and Regulatory Council, Perchlorate: Overview of Issues, Status and Remedial Options (2005), http://cluin.org/contaminantfocus/default.focus/sec/perchlorate/cat/Overview (accessed Sept. 4, 2006).
26. 33 U.S.C. § 1323(a).
27. Stephen Dycus, National Defense and the Environment 46–47 (1996) (discussing *Weinberger v. Romero-Barcelo*, 456 U.S. 305 [1982]).
28. 42 U.S.C. § 7418(b).
29. Exec. Order No. 12,244, 45 Fed. Reg. 66,443 (1980).
30. 42 U.S.C. § 6961(a).
31. *Id.*
32. Presidential Determination No. 95-45, 60 Fed. Reg. 52,823 (Oct. 10, 1995).

33. Kasza v. Browner, 133 F.3d 1159, 1173 (9th Cir. 1998).

34. Colonel E. G. Willard, Lieutenant Colonel Tom Zimmerman, Lieutenant Colonel Eric Bee, *Environmental Law and National Security: Can Existing Exemption in Environmental Laws Preserve DoD Training and Operational prerogatives without New Legislation?* 54 A.F. L. REV. 65, 87 (2004).

35. GENERAL ACCOUNTING OFFICE, MILITARY TRAINING: DOD LACKS A COMPREHENSIVE PLAN TO MANAGE ENCROACHMENT ON TRAINING RANGES, REPORT TO CONGRESSIONAL REQUESTERS, June 11, 2002.

36. Statement of Deputy Undersecretary of Defense (Installations and Environment) Raymond F. Dubois Jr. before the House Committee on Resources: Subcommittee on Fisheries, Conservation, Wildlife and Oceans, June 13, 2002, www.defenselink.mil/dodgc/olc/docs/test02-06-13DuBois.rtf (accessed Nov. 11, 2005).

37. GENERAL ACCOUNTING OFFICE, MILITARY TRAINING at 5–8.

38. *Id.* at 9.

39. *Id.* at 15.

40. *Id.*

41. Opening Statement of U.S. Senator Bob Smith, *The Range Readiness and Preservation Initiative of the Department of Defense*, U.S. Senate Committee on Environment and Public Works, July 9, 2002, http://epw.senate.gov/107th/smi_070902.htm (accessed Nov. 11, 2005).

42. 16 U.S.C. §§ 703–12.

43. 39 Stat. 1702 (1916).

44. Center for Biological Diversity v. Pirie, 191 F. Supp. 2d 161 (D. D.C. 2002).

45. Alex Beehler and Ann Erin Mercer, *Sea Change at Defense*, ENVTL. FORUM 22–24 (Sept./Oct. 2005).

46. Staff of the Attorneys General of Colorado, Idaho, Utah, and Washington, *Readiness and Range Preservation Initiative (RRPI): Myth and Fact*, response to the Department of Defense's position paper, Apr. 2004, www.cpeo.org/dodexemptions/myth%20rebuttal%204-2-04.doc (accessed Nov. 11, 2005).

47. *Id.* at 1.

48. *Id.* at 2–3.

49. See, e.g., Martin O. Sabo, *Wrapping Extremist Proposals in Patriotic Bunting*, MINNEAPOLIS STAR TRIBUNE, Mar. 23, 2003.

50. Stephen Dycus, *Behind Veil of Terrorism, DoD Wants Blanket Exemptions*, ENVTL. FORUM 23 (Sept./Oct. 2005).

51. Christine Todd Whitman, EPA administrator, letter to Donald Rumsfeld, secretary of Defense, Mar. 10, 2003.

52. *Id.*

53. Donald Rumsfeld, letter to Christine Todd Whitman, Apr. 15, 2003.

54. Pub. L. No. 107-314, Div. A, Title III, Subtitle B, § 315, 116 Stat. 2509.

55. 16 U.S.C. § 1533(a)(3)(B).

56. 16 U.S.C. § 670a.

57. 16 U.S.C. §§ 1361–1421(h).

58. Pub. L. No. 108-136, § 319.

59. 16 U.S.C. § 1371 et seq.

60. EUGENE H. BUCK, CONGRESSIONAL RESEARCH SERVICE, ACTIVE MILITARY SONAR AND MARINE MAMMALS: EVENTS AND REFERENCES 1 (Nov. 3, 2005).

61. *Id.*

62. *Id.* at 2.

63. *Id.* at 3.

64. *Id.*

65. *Id.*

66. *Id.* at 4.

67. *Id.* at 5.

68. Natural Resources Defense Council v. U.S. Department of the Navy, U.S. Dist. Lexis 26360 (2002).

69. Natural Resources Defense Council v. Evans, 232 F. Supp. 2d 1003 (N.D. Calif. 2002).

70. BUCK, ACTIVE MILITARY SONAR, supra note 60, at 6.

71. Natural Resources Defense Council v. Evans, 279 F. Supp. 2d 1129 (N.D. Calif. 2003).

72. Hawaii County Green Party v. Evans, C-03-0078 (N.D. Calif., Jan. 24, 2003).

73. Cetacean Community v. Bush, 386 F.3d 1169 (9th Cir. 2004).

74. BUCK, ACTIVE MILITARY SONAR, supra note 60, at 10–11.

75. *Id.* at 11.

76. Natural Resources Defense Council v. Winter, C-06-4131 (C.D. Calif., July 3, 2006).

77. Natural Resources Defense Council, *Sonar Lawsuit Settlement: Navy Will Limit Needless Harm to Whales*, July 7, 2006, www.nrdc.org/media/pressreleases/060707.asp.

5

Land Acquisition through Military Land Withdrawals

Two trends in military land use dominated the second half of the twentieth century. More sophisticated, longer range weapon systems and the Cold War drove a need for training lands well beyond the capacity of the United States' traditional cavalry garrisons of a century prior. Inevitably, the government turned to the western public lands to satisfy the need for increased training space. Conversely, the end of the Cold War during the late 1980s brought on an era of "downsizing" in the military that included disposal of the surplus military infrastructure that had been built up during World War II and the Cold War—although the need for large tracts of training lands continued because of long-range weaponry.

Military Land Withdrawals

The Army's Fort Bliss, Texas, and the Bureau of Land Management (BLM) have shared oversight of the McGregor Range, New Mexico, since 1957. The McGregor Range consists of over 608,000 acres of land withdrawn from the public domain.[1] The withdrawal of public domain land for military use, under which the BLM and Fort Bliss share management of the range, was most recently renewed by Congress in the Military Lands Withdrawal Act of 1999 (MLWA).[2] The two very different federal agencies managed the land since 1990 in accordance with a memorandum of understanding (MOU) between them.[3] The MOU gave Fort Bliss priority use of the range for military purposes. The BLM, however, managed the nonmilitary activities on the range, such as cattle grazing and recreation, subject to the Army's concurrence.[4]

The Department of Defense (DOD) manages millions of acres across the nation in conjunction with the BLM pursuant to various temporary land withdrawals. The most significant of the land withdrawals were created under the MLWA of 1986,[5] which officially established six large military training and testing areas including the Navy's 21,000-acre Bravo-20 Bombing Range in Nevada, the Air Force's 2.9 million-acre Nellis Range in Nevada, its 2.6 million-acre Barry M. Goldwater Range in Arizona, and about 900,000 acres in Army training areas in Alaska.[6] The Department of Defense has also benefited from many smaller withdrawals, which are considered "administrative withdrawals" that do not require formal congressional approval for renewal.[7] Under the Engle Act of 1958,[8] land withdrawals of more than 5,000 acres require such formal congressional approval.[9]

Under the MLWA of 1986, the Army, Navy, and Air Force were charged with submitting applications to the BLM for continued withdrawal of these large areas of withdrawn lands beyond the year 2001.[10] Under the MLWA of 1986, BLM was required then to process the applications for renewal in light of its own regulations, but only Congress could extend or renew the withdrawals.[11] As part of their applications for renewal, the services were required to provide a draft environmental impact statement (DEIS) for each withdrawal the services intended to renew.[12] Under the MLWA of 1999, the services will have to go through a similar process to retain training lands beyond 2021 or 2026, depending on the site.[13]

Military land withdrawals created unique opportunities and challenges for interagency cooperation. They allowed the BLM to manage natural resources in conjunction with military testing and training. The land withdrawals also presented some unique management challenges for both agencies. Assessing cumulative environmental impacts of very different types of activities managed by two different agencies, for instance, wasn't easily accomplished. In addition, it is difficult to picture two agencies with more different management approaches than the BLM and the Army, Navy, or Air Force. Yet, in spite of occasional disagreements, the relationship has arguably worked to the overall benefit of both partners and the public. Although the MLWA forced the BLM to surrender management supremacy of public lands to the military services, its role in working with the military in cooperatively managing resources and in processing renewal applications has made the BLM a key partner in the country's national defense.

The Historical Framework for the MLWA of 1986

Under the property clause of the U.S. Constitution, Congress has authority to govern the uses of public lands.[14] The Constitution provided that Congress could "dispose of and make all needful Rules and Regulations respecting the Territory or other Property belonging to the United States."[15] In addition, the Enclave Clause of the Constitution gave Congress the "power to exercise exclusive Legislation in all Cases whatsoever . . . over all Places purchased by the Consent of the Legislature of the State in which the Same shall be, for the Erection of Forts, Magazines, Arsenals, dock-Yards, and other needful Buildings."[16] Congress's authority has been applied broadly, with the U.S. Supreme Court determining several times that "the power over public lands thus entrusted to Congress is without limitation."[17] This congressional power has applied not only to lands acquired from states but also to public domain land retained by the federal government as each new state was admitted to the union.[18]

The president, however, has long held exercised authority to withdraw or reserve land whenever Congress has allowed him to do so. Generally, a land withdrawal exempts public lands from development except in accordance with the terms of the withdrawal. In *United States v. Midwest Oil Co.*,[19] the U.S. Supreme Court in 1915 upheld the traditional practice of the president, with the acquiescence of Congress, of creating land withdrawals by executive order.[20] The Court acknowledged the many withdrawals by executive order prior to 1910, including "109 Executive orders establishing or enlarging military reservations and setting apart land for water, timber, fuel, hay, signal stations, target ranges, and rights of way for use in connection with military reservations."[21] The Court also recognized that Congress had been informed of the naval oil reserve withdrawal in controversy and had not objected. "Its silence was acquiescence," the Court concluded. "Its acquiescence was equivalent to consent to continue the practice until the power was revoked by some subsequent action by Congress."[22]

Congress passed the Pickett Act of 1910 in an effort to limit the broad withdrawal power of the president.[23] The Pickett Act authorized the president to temporarily withdraw land "from settlement, location, sale, or entry" and to "reserve the same for water-power sites, irrigation, classification of lands, or other public purposes to be specified in the orders of withdrawals."[24] The Pickett Act also placed limits on the president's power, however, by providing that lands withdrawn under the Act "shall at all times be open to exploration, discovery, occupation, and purchase under the mining laws of the United States, so far as the same apply to metalliferous minerals."[25] However, the Pickett Act did not stop the president from making land withdrawals. In 1941, the U.S. Attorney General interpreted the Act as limiting only "temporary" land, which did not affect the president's nonstatutory authority to make "permanent" withdrawals.[26]

Unless withdrawn, management of the public lands was historically given to federal agencies upon the assent of Congress. For instance, the Taylor

Grazing Act of 1934 gave the secretary of the Interior authority to promulgate regulations to oversee grazing on the public lands.[27] The public domain lands addressed under the Taylor Grazing Act were managed by the Department of the Interior's Grazing Service until 1946, when the BLM was created from the Grazing Service and the separate General Land Office. But withdrawn lands were not subject to management by the BLM unless otherwise noted in the instrument for withdrawal.

Land withdrawals prior to 1958, including military land withdrawals, could be unlimited in duration and size. The Engle Act changed that paradigm. In adopting the Engle Act in 1958, Congress reserved for itself the ability to create withdrawals greater than 5,000 acres.[28] Then in 1976, Congress adopted the Federal Land Policy and Management Act (FLPMA), which delegated to the Department of the Interior the ability to create withdrawals of 5,000 acres or less and is also considered the organic act for the BLM.[29]

FLPMA gave the Department of the Interior the authority to "make, modify, extend or revoke withdrawals" of federal land.[30] FLPMA thus authorized an administrative process for handling smaller land withdrawals.[31] It also mandated the secretary of the Interior to review all existing withdrawals of public lands within Arizona, California, Colorado, Idaho, Montana, Nevada, New Mexico, Oregon, Utah, Washington, and Wyoming within fifteen years if the withdrawals closed the lands to appropriation under the Mining Law of 1872 or to leasing under the Mineral Leasing Act of 1920.[32] The review was intended to determine whether the withdrawals were still required for their stated purposes.[33] The Department of Interior's regulations provide a process to consider applications for withdrawals and do not distinguish between the application and renewal of administrative withdrawals under FLPMA and congressional withdrawals.[34] Thus, agencies seeking congressional withdrawals follow the same FLPMA application and review procedures.

The MLWA of 1986

The MLWA of 1986, with respect to McGregor Range, New Mexico, corrected a ten-year absence of congressional action. While Congress considered the Army's request to renew the 1957 withdrawal of the McGregor Range, which was filed on December 31, 1976, Congress provided no further guidance with respect to the use of McGregor Range.[35] Other military installations and facilities of the other military services had been operating with a similar lack of guidance.[36] Congress finally filled the void created by the lack of guidance by passage of the MLWA of 1986, which was in effect for fifteen years.[37] The MLWA of 1986 ensured that military use of the withdrawn public domain lands was then consistent with both the Engle Act and FLPMA's withdrawal provision.[38]

The MLWA of 1986 provided that each of the six major military withdrawals[39] were "withdrawn from all forms of appropriation under the public land laws (including the mining laws and the mineral leasing and the geothermal leasing laws)."[40] Each of the withdrawals identified specific military purposes for which the lands are to be used. For instance, the Navy's Bravo-20 Bombing Range in Nevada was reserved for "testing and training for aerial bombing, missile firing, and tactical maneuvering and air support."[41] Further, the Nellis Air Force Range in Nevada was reserved for use as "an armament and high-hazard testing area" as well as for "training for aerial gunnery, rocketry, electronic warfare, and tactical maneuvering and air support."[42] The McGregor Range in New Mexico was reserved for "training and weapons testing."[43]

In addition to the specific purposes identified for the withdrawals, each withdrawal provided that the lands could be used for "other defense-related purposes consistent with the purposes specified in this withdrawal."[44] To use withdrawn lands for such "additional military uses," however, the military service concerned was required to notify the BLM.[45] The notification was required to "indicate the additional use or uses involved, the proposed duration of such uses," as well as the extent to which the additional military uses would call for "additional or more stringent conditions or restrictions" to be "imposed on otherwise-permitted nonmilitary uses of the withdrawn land or portions thereof."[46]

The MLWA of 1986 also provided that existing rights on the withdrawn lands would be left intact.[47] It also specified that lands within the Bravo-20 Bombing Range controlled by the Bureau of Reclamation for "flooding, overflow, and seepage purposes" were not affected by the withdrawal.[48] In addition, the Act provided that lands on the McGregor Range managed under Section 603 of FLPMA "shall continue to be managed under that section until Congress determines otherwise."[49] Section 603 outlined the BLM's Wilderness Study Area requirements.[50] An area on McGregor Range known as Culp Canyon was designated as a Wilderness Study Area and continued under that designation. As such, the BLM and the Army were required to maintain the area in a state "where the earth and its community of life are untrammeled by man, where man himself is a visitor who does not remain."[51]

The MLWA of 1986 also required the BLM to oversee the nonmilitary uses of the withdrawn lands pursuant to FLPMA and other applicable laws, including the Recreation Use of Wildlife Areas Act of 1962.[52] The Act provided that the BLM could manage the range in such a way that permitted the continuation of grazing, protection of wildlife and wildlife habitat, control of predatory and other animals, recreation, and control of brush and range fires.[53] The MLWA specified that all nonmilitary activities were subject to conditions and restrictions "as may be necessary to permit the military use of such lands for the purposes specified in or authorized pursuant to this act."[54] The BLM could authorize use of the withdrawn land "only with the concurrence" of the military service concerned.[55] Also, each of the military services could close areas within the withdrawals when "military operations, public safety, or national security" require it, although such closures are limited to the "minimum areas and periods . . . required to carry out" the operation requiring the closure.[56] The BLM was required to create management plans, in cooperation with the military services, for the withdrawn lands.[57] In addition, the MLWA of 1986 required the BLM and the military services to enter into agreements to implement the management plans.[58] The cooperative, multiple-use management scheme established under the MLWA of 1986 was reincorporated into the MLWA of 1999.[59]

The MLWA of 1986 also specified that its withdrawals did not include any reserved water rights[60] and that hunting, fishing, and trapping would be in accordance with Title 10, Section 2671.[61] Those provisions of the MLWA of 1986 ensured that the withdrawn lands would be effectively managed under state water and game laws. The MLWA of 1986 also required that the BLM and the military services determine, at least every five years, which, if any, of the withdrawn lands would be "suitable" for opening under the Mining Law of 1872, the Mineral Leasing Act of 1920, the Mineral Leasing Act for Acquired Lands of 1947, or the Geothermal Steam Act of 1970.[62] The Act also required that mining claims were subject to the terms of FLPMA and that any patent issued as a result of mineral development would convey title only to the minerals, keeping title to the surface vested in the United States.[63] These provisions in the MLWA of 1986, carried forward into the MLWA of 1999, ensured that the withdrawals caused the minimum impact possible to development of private interests while maintaining military priority over the withdrawn lands.

Interagency Cooperation under the MLWA of 1986

The MLWA of 1986 required considerable teamwork between each of the military services and the BLM. It is difficult to imagine any two federal agencies as fundamentally different, however, as a military service, such as the Army, and the BLM. The Army, despite its far-flung global operations, is a highly centralized organization, with the entire agency focusing on one mission—preparation for war fighting. To be ready for war, all parts of the whole must work in coordination with all others. Major decisions, therefore, are centralized in Washington, D.C.

By contrast, the BLM is decentralized, with state and local offices having significant autonomy within the agency because of the diversity of the BLM's customer base. The BLM must continually seek to balance fiercely competing interests for any particular resource, which is exactly the opposite of the military's singleness of purpose. BLM officials, more so than the Army, work to cultivate local followings. Ranchers who graze their cattle on BLM-administered lands become, in effect, constituents of the BLM. On the occasions when the BLM and the Army disagreed over management of McGregor Range withdrawal lands, the Fort Bliss commanding general was flooded with mail from BLM supporters.[64]

The military and the BLM nevertheless found a way to work together to manage withdrawn land on McGregor Range.[65] The Army and the BLM were able to negotiate a memorandum of understanding (MOU) regarding management of McGregor Range that closely defined the responsibilities of both parties regarding range management.[66] As a result, McGregor Range became a good example of multiple-use management. It provided training space for air defense artillery units, including Patriot missile units, and maneuver areas for ground troops. Concurrently, the range provided lucrative grazing leases for the BLM, which reached as high as $15 per animal unit month.[67] The range also provided recreation opportunities for hunters and hikers.

Under the MOU between the Army at Fort Bliss and the BLM, the BLM served as the lead agency for supervising public use of the withdrawn lands.[68] The Army was entitled to 10 percent, based on the approximate proportion of its fee-owned lands to the entire range, of any income derived from public use of the range.[69] BLM was also responsible for managing salable and leasable mineral programs, vegetation management, and livestock grazing.[70] Livestock grazing was "based on the principles of multiple use and sustained yield."[71] In addition, BLM was designated in the MOU as the lead agency for recreational use of the range, including hunting.[72] Under the MOU, Fort Bliss concurrence was required for any nonmilitary use of the range.[73]

The MOU between Fort Bliss and BLM also identified the parties' relative responsibilities for compliance with the National Environmental Policy Act (NEPA),[74] the Endangered Species Act (ESA),[75] and the National Historic Preservation Act (NHPA) for activities on the range.[76] It also defined each agency's role in fire suppression[77] and law enforcement.[78] The MOU provided for periodic meetings between the agencies and a process for resolving disputes between the parties.[79] The MOU provided a successful framework for the BLM-Army relationship on McGregor Range. To carry out its training mission, the Army used its own military training plans and operating procedures, while the BLM followed its Resource Management Plan to pursue its multiple-use objectives.[80]

With respect to management of military withdrawal lands throughout the nation under the 1986 Act, some commentators actually applauded the military's stewardship. "It is clear that the military is actually a reasonably good partner in environmental conscious land management, as measured both comparatively and by absolute standards," wrote commentator Darrin Hostetler. "The military aids in the preservation of public lands in ways both active and passive by taking affirmative pro-preservation measures and by simply holding its vast land properties secure from alternative uses."[81] The BLM, on the other hand, was criticized for "failing to achieve environmental goals" under the joint management of withdrawal lands.[82]

Renewal of the 1986 Withdrawals

Approaching the end of the term of the 1986 land withdrawals, many were bracing for a difficult fight between the military services, the BLM, and stakeholders. "The legislative fight over withdrawn lands is the wrong war, with the wrong enemy, at the wrong time," wrote Hostetler.[83] "The battlefield upon which the upcoming legal and policy war is to take place, the floor and hearing rooms of Congress, presents profound disadvantages for environmentalists and the military alike. Congress makes an especially poor and inefficient referee in this dispute."[84]

During the late 1990s, the military withdrawals demanded close cooperation between the military services and the BLM in considering the renewal requests for the withdrawals—a process that will be repeated as we approach 2021 or 2026, depending on the installation, when the MLWA of 1999 expires. The Engle Act gave Congress the sole authority to continue renewals of withdrawals such as those created under the MLWA of 1986 and 1999.[85] The Engle Act requires the following basic information for applications for withdrawal: (1) the name of the agency; (2) a detailed description of the location of the property; (3) the physical characteristics of the property, including gross land and water acreage; (4) the proposed use of the withdrawn land; (5) whether the planned use "will result in contamination of any or all of the requested withdrawal" and "whether such contamination will be permanent or temporary"; (6) the period during which the proposed withdrawal would be in effect; (7) whether the proposed use would compromise use of natural resources on the land such as timber, mineral, grazing, fish and wildlife, and so forth; and (8) whether water rights will be required to support the proposed use of the withdrawn land.[86] While the Engle Act contains no specific conditions for renewal, both the BLM and the military have inferred that requirements for renewal are similar to those of an initial withdrawal.[87]

The MLWA of 1986 required the military services to notify the Department of the Interior by November 6, 1998—three years prior to expiration of the withdrawals—whether the services would seek extensions.[88] This requirement was consistent with FLPMA's withdrawal provision, which requires the Department of Interior to process withdrawal applications, even in situations in which Congress would make the final determination regarding withdrawal.[89] The BLM was then required to process the renewal applications in accordance with its regulatory procedures.[90] The applications included information regarding cultural resources, roadless areas, mineral resources, a biological assessment, an economic impact analysis, and a summary of public participation.[91] These materials could be submitted with the environmental impact statement (EIS) or separately and incorporated by reference.[92] The process was expected to take some time, with a smooth process essential for the applications to be considered by Congress prior to the expiration of the 1986 withdrawals.

In case of a disagreement between the applicants (the military services) and the BLM, the BLM's regulations provide a brief dispute resolution process. Under the regulations, the BLM would prepare preliminary findings and recommendations, which would be submitted to the secretary of the Interior after the agencies had an opportunity to discuss their differences.[93]

The MLWA of 1986 also required that the military services each publish a draft environmental impact statement (DEIS) for each of the withdrawn areas by November 6, 1998.[94] Under the Council on Environmental Quality (CEQ) regulations, the BLM was generally considered to be a cooperating agency to each of the environmental studies. The roles of lead and cooperating agencies, however, were loosely defined in the CEQ's NEPA regulations. The regulations required that a cooperating agency would participate in the NEPA process "at the earliest possible time," participating in scoping, providing information and assistance upon request of the lead agency, and using its own funds for analyses it requests.[95] An agency requested to be a cooperating agency could also decline to participate if other program commitments would not allow it.[96] In addition, prior to the expiration date of the withdrawals, each of the services were required to conduct a public hearing on the DEIS for each withdrawal.[97] The BLM would likely have participated in each of those public hearings as well; however, such participation was unnecessary as passage of the MLWA of 1999 occurred far in advance of the 2001 expiration of the 1986 withdrawals.[98]

To better define the roles of the agencies in the MLWA of 1986 renewal process, Fort Bliss and the BLM entered into a memorandum of agreement (MOA).[99] The MOA outlined the responsibilities of cooperating agencies on the EIS, the BLM's requirements in light of the Interior Department's renewal regulations, and dispute resolution procedures.[100] Most significantly, the MOA defined the scope of the analysis to be accomplished in the renewal EIS. Specifically, the primary purpose of the EIS was to provide information to Congress regarding various withdrawal scenarios such as "continued withdrawal, the alternative of no withdrawal, and all other reasonable alternatives which may include boundary and time adjustments to the existing withdrawal."[101] The agencies also agreed in the MOA that a separate EIS being prepared to study Fort Bliss's "Ongoing Missions and Master Plan" would be incorporated by reference into the renewal EIS. That EIS discussed and analyzed all significant ongoing and proposed activities on Fort Bliss.[102] This approach not only gave the public opportunities to comment on proposed and ongoing training activities on Fort Bliss but also allowed the public a separate opportunity to provide input to congressional decision making.

As discussed in earlier chapters, Fort Bliss also had requirements driven by the NHPA and ESA as all federal facilities have. Under Section 106 of the NHPA, any federal "undertaking" triggers a consultation requirement with state historic preservation officers (SHPOs) and the federal government's Advisory Council on Historic Preservation (ACHP) regarding the future of districts, sites, buildings, structures, and objects that are in or eligible for the National Register of Historic Places.[103] Section 7 of ESA required Fort Bliss officials to consult with the U.S. Fish and Wildlife Service to determine whether an activity will subject an endangered species or its critical habitat to "jeopardy."[104] Fort Bliss satisfied the NHPA and ESA requirements concurrently with preparation of the Ongoing Mission and Master Plan EIS.

During the application process, the military branches and the BLM worked out tensions that arose because of the agencies' different missions. An early conflict between the BLM and Fort Bliss, for instance, regarded the status of Otero Mesa and the Sacramento foothills, which were prime grazing land that constituted the main focus of the BLM's activity on the range, under a possible continued withdrawal. Because of the competing interests between the agencies, the BLM early in the process publicly stated that it would oppose continued withdrawal of those areas—that the areas should instead be placed under the BLM's exclusive control.[105] Fort Bliss disagreed, because the military expected to have a continuing need for these areas. Ultimately, the MLWA of 1999 included the continued withdrawal of the Otero Mesa consistent with Fort Bliss's continued training needs.[106]

The MLWA of 1999, adopted October 5, 1999, extended for years the terms of withdrawal for Naval Air Station Fallon Ranges, Nevada; Nellis Air Force Range, Nevada; Fort Greely and Fort Wainwright Training Ranges, Alaska; and McGregor Range, Fort Bliss, New Mexico. The commencement date for those withdrawals was set as November 6, 2001, with the Fallon and Nellis withdrawals running for twenty years—terminating in 2021—and the withdrawals for the Army ranges in Alaska and New Mexico running for twenty-five years until 2026. An application for renewal of each withdrawal would have to be submitted three years prior to their termination, or November 6, 2003, if the service secretaries determine that continued military withdrawal will be necessary.[107] The services are required to "maintain a program of decontamination" on the withdrawn ranges "to the extent funds are available."[108] If the military services do not wish to extend the withdrawals, the BLM will have an option to take the lands but will not be required to take administrative control of the lands if decontamination to a degree sufficient to be used as public land is not economically feasible.[109] If BLM does not take withdrawn lands back because they're too contaminated, the military services are required to take action to warn the public of the contamination, to conduct no further activities on the lands "except in connection with decontamination," and to submit a report to the Department of the Interior and Congress on actions taken to decontaminate the lands.[110]

The MLWA of 1999 also continued the withdrawal of the Barry M. Goldwater Range in Arizona for twenty-five years but placed additional management responsibilities on the Air Force and Navy, which were to control the East and West ranges, respectively.[111] Congress imposed additional management requirements because of the environmental sensitivity of the area, which includes the Cabeza Prieta National Wildlife Refuge. The Department of the Interior is to manage the wildlife refuge.[112] The Air Force and Navy are required to manage the ranges in accordance with an integrated natural resources management plan.[113] If the BLM believes the Navy or Air Force are not managing according to the management plan, however, there is a process established in the legislation that allows the BLM to assume management responsibility for natural resources on the ranges.[114]

The Process Repeats

With approximately seven million acres of public domain land being used both for military and nonmilitary purposes, the military services and the BLM of necessity learned to cooperate closely in land management. Despite the occasional head butting between the agencies because of their conflicting missions, the Engle Act and the MLWA made it possible for the BLM and the military services to extend land resources beyond those uses ordinarily seen on public domain lands. The relationship provided valuable training and testing space for the military while continuing to allow the BLM to apply multiple use, sustained yield principles to nonmilitary land uses. As a result, the BLM established itself as an effective partner to the military in managing the lands. But the military requirement for massive tracts of training lands is not likely to disappear. As the 1999 withdrawals approach their expiration dates in 2021 and 2026, however, the military services and the BLM will again have to enter the complex process of withdrawal renewal, which requires significant coordination on numerous environmental documents. Despite the occasional tension that the sometimes conflicting missions of the agencies cause—the military's need for training lands and the BLM's mandate to manage public lands—the MLWA of 1999 will again require those agencies, all within the executive branch of government, to again work out their differences. To mitigate some of the inevitable delays and difficulties in administratively processing the applications, the agencies should begin planning for the renewals well before the expiration dates of the present withdrawals.

Notes

1. Public Land Order No. 1470. The 1957 order was for an initial period of ten years, with an additional term of ten years at the option of the Army. The Army exercised its option and also submitted an application for renewal of the withdrawal on December 31, 1976, which Congress did not act upon until 1986.

2. Military Lands Withdrawal Act of 1999, Pub. L. 106-65 (1999). For a discussion of the land withdrawal prior to the 1999 Act, see William A. Wilcox Jr. and Andrew J. Vliet III, *The Engle Act and Military Land Withdrawals: A Blueprint for Inter-Agency Cooperation*, 32 LAND & WATER L. REV. 461 (1997). See also Darrin Hostetler, *The Wrong War, With the Wrong Enemy, at the Wrong Time: The Coming Battle over the Military Land Withdrawal Act and an Experiment in Privatizing the Regulation of Public Lands*, 29 ENVTL. L. 303 (1999).

3. Memorandum of Understanding between U.S. Department of the Interior Bureau of Land Management, New Mexico, and U.S. Department of the Army, Headquarters, U.S. Army Air Defense Artillery Center and Fort Bliss, Fort Bliss, Texas, concerning Policies, Procedures, and Responsibilities related to Land Use Planning and Resource Management of McGregor Range, March 1, 1990.

4. *Id.* at III(A).

5. Military Lands Withdrawal Act of 1986, Pub. L. 99-606 (1986).

6. *Id.*

7. Shelly J. Smith et al., *Maintaining Army Readiness: The Status of NEPA Documentation for Renewal of Withdrawn Military Lands* (prepared for the American Defense Preparedness Association's 22nd Environmental Symposium and Exhibition, Mar. 18–21, 1996).

8. 43 U.S.C. §§ 155–58.

9. 43 U.S.C. § 156.

10. Military Lands Withdrawal Act of 1986, supra note 2, at § 8(a).

11. *Id.* § 5(c).

12. *Id.* § 5(b).
13. Military Lands Withdrawal Act of 1999, §§ 3015–16.
14. U.S. Const. art. IV, § 3, cl. 2.
15. *Id.*
16. U.S. Const. art. I, § 8, cl. 17.
17. See, e.g., Kleppe v. New Mexico, 426 U.S. 529, 539 (1976) (quoting United States v. San Francisco, 310 U.S. 16, 20 [1949]).
18. See, e.g., Pollard v. Hagan, 44 U.S. 212 (1845).
19. United States v. Midwest Oil Co., 236 U.S. 459 (1915).
20. *Id.* at 483.
21. *Id.* at 470.
22. *Id.* at 481.
23. Pickett Act, 36 Stat. 847, ch. 421 (June 25, 1990), §§ 1–2, repealed by 43 U.S.C. § 704(a), 90 Stat. 2744, 2792.
24. *Id.* § 1.
25. *Id.* § 2.
26. Charles F. Wheatley Jr., Study of Withdrawals and Reservations of Public Domain Lands 5 (1969).
27. Taylor Grazing Act of 1934, ch. 865, § 1, 48 Stat. 1269, codified as amended at 43 U.S.C. (1988), § 315.
28. 43 U.S.C. § 156.
29. 43 U.S.C. § 1714.
30. 43 U.S.C. § 1714(a).
31. According to the BLM, there are currently fifteen administrative withdrawals with specific termination dates, seven concerning military installations and the rest concerning U.S. Army Corps of Engineers civil works (Smith et al., *Maintaining Army Readiness*, supra note 7, at 2).
32. 43 U.S.C. § 1714(l)(1).
33. 43 U.S.C. § 1714(l)(2).
34. 43 C.F.R. (1981) pt. 2300.
35. Wilcox and Vliet, *The Engle Act*, supra note 2, at 465.
36. *Id.*
37. Military Lands Withdrawal Act of 1986, supra note 2, at § 5(a).
38. See 43 U.S.C. § 156; 43 U.S.C. § 1714.
39. See Military Lands Withdrawal Act of 1986, supra note 2, and accompanying text.
40. *Id.*, supra note 2, at § 1.
41. *Id.* § 1(a)(1)(A).
42. *Id.* § 1(b)(1)(A), (B).
43. *Id.* § 1(d)(1)(A).
44. *Id.* § 1.
45. *Id.* § 3(f).
46. *Id.*
47. *Id.* § 1.
48. *Id.* § 1(a)(3).

49. *Id.* § 1(d)(3).

50. 43 U.S.C. § 1782.

51. See 16 U.S.C. § 1131(c). McGregor Range has other unexpected environmental treasures as well. An abandoned Army shed on the range, for instance, is home to the world's largest colony of pallid bats. While the bats are not a listed species, biologists are concerned about their disappearing habitat. Fort Bliss, therefore, dedicated the shed to the preservation of the bat colony. Juan A. Lozano, *Bat House: McGregor Range Is Home to Large Colony of Pallid Bats*, El Paso Herald-Post, Sept. 14, 1995, at B-1.

52. Military Lands Withdrawal Act of 1986, supra note 2, at § 3(a)(1). The Act further specified, however, that lands located in the Desert National Wildlife Range in Nevada and the Cabeza Prieta National Wildlife Refuge in Arizona were to be managed under the National Wildlife Refuge System Administration Act of 1966.

53. *Id.* § 3(a)(2).

54. *Id.* § 3(a)(3)(A).

55. *Id.* § 3(a)(3)(B).

56. *Id.* § 3(b).

57. *Id.* § 3(c).

58. *Id.* § 3(e).

59. Military Lands Withdrawal Act of 1999, § 3014.

60. Military Lands Withdrawal Act of 1986, § 10.

61. *Id.* § 11.

62. *Id.* § 12(a).

63. *Id.* §§ 12(f), (g).

64. Unfortunately, these disagreements occasionally surfaced in local newspapers. See, e.g., *BLM, Army at Odds over Grazing*, Las Cruces (N.M.) Sun-News, Sept. 7, 1995, at A1. BLM planned to issue three-year grazing leases on an area covering about 33,000 acres of McGregor Range. The Army disagreed, however, preferring to keep the land available for possible military use, because Armywide realignment was making it difficult to gauge future space needs, and approximately 117,000 acres of the range were already cleared for grazing. The two agencies eventually agreed to allow eighteen-month leases.

65. Because of mission requirements, the degree to which the military services and the BLM must cooperate at other withdrawal locations varies.

66. See Memorandum of Understanding, supra note 3.

67. Leases on McGregor Range are awarded by competitive bid, which is unique among BLM administered lands in the West. This system is a result of the original withdrawal in 1957, under which the Army discontinued grazing. The Army reinstated grazing in the late 1960s, and BLM assumed management of the program. By agreement between the agencies, leases on McGregor Range are awarded competitively for short periods of time, usually nine or eighteen months.

68. Memorandum of Understanding, supra note 3, at 2.

69. *Id.* at 3.

70. *Id.* at 4–7.

71. *Id.* at 6.

72. *Id.* at 14–15.

73. *Id.* at 1–2.

74. *Id.*

75. *Id.* at 10.

76. *Id.* at 11–13.

77. *Id.* at 16–17.

78. *Id.* at 18.

79. *Id.* at 20–21. The dispute resolution process required, in general, that disputes be resolved at the lowest possible level and, if necessary, elevated to higher levels of management within the agencies (21).

80. U.S. Department of Interior, BLM Las Cruces District Office, Caballo Resource Area, *Resource Management Plan Amendment: McGregor Range* (1990).

81. Hostetler, *The Wrong War*, supra note 2, at 316–17.

82. *Id.* at 319 (citing GENERAL ACCOUNTING OFFICE, NATURAL RESOURCES: DEFENSE AND INTERIOR CAN BETTER MANAGE LAND WITHDRAWN FOR MILITARY USE [1994]).

83. Hostetler, *The Wrong War*, supra note 2, at 306.

84. *Id.* at 323.

85. 43 U.S.C. § 156.

86. 43 U.S.C. § 157.

87. *Id.*

88. Military Lands Withdrawal Act of 1986, supra note 2, at § 8(a).

89. 43 U.S.C. § 1714(c) (establishing procedures and providing for congressional review and approval of all withdrawals over 5,000 acres).

90. 43 C.F.R. pts. 2300–2310.

91. 43 C.F.R. § 2310.3-2(b)(3).

92. *Id.*

93. 43 C.F.R. § 2310.3-2(e).

94. Military Lands Withdrawal Act of 1986, supra note 2, at § 5(b). Congress apparently anticipated that the BLM would require some time to process the applications and that Congress itself would need time to act on the proposed withdrawals.

95. 40 C.F.R. § 1501.6(b).

96. *Id.* § 1501.6(c).

97. Military Lands Withdrawal Act of 1986, supra note 2, at § 5(b).

98. Military Lands Withdrawal Act of 1999 was enacted on October 5, 1999.

99. Memorandum of Agreement between Fort Bliss, U.S. Army, and New Mexico State Office, Bureau of Land Management, U.S.D.I. for the Renewal Application for the Withdrawal of McGregor Range, New Mexico (1996).

100. *Id.*

101. *Id.* § II(1).

102. Fort Bliss includes about 400,000 acres of land in addition to McGregor Range. These other areas include the "main cantonment area" where the post headquarters is located adjacent to the city of El Paso, Texas.

103. 16 U.S.C. § 470f.

104. 16 U.S.C. § 1536.

105. See, e.g., Daniel Perez, *Fort Bliss Wants Firing Ranges Intact*, EL PASO TIMES, July 4, 1996, at 1.

106. Military Lands Withdrawal Act of 1999, § 3011(d).
107. *Id.* § 3016.
108. *Id.* § 3017(a).
109. *Id.* § 3017(d).
110. *Id.* § 3017(e).
111. *Id.* § 3031(a).
112. *Id.* § 3032(b).
113. *Id.* § 3031(b).
114. *Id.* § 3031(b)(7).

6

Base Realignments and Closures

As a counterpoint to the expansion of the military's training and testing capabilities through public land withdrawals, base realignments and closures (BRAC) were implemented by the federal government in the wake of the Cold War. The latest round, "BRAC '05" recently reached its political conclusion, and community leaders in localities affected by the BRAC round will look beyond fighting closures of installations in their communities to exploring how those closed installations can best be exploited to strengthen the economic health of their communities. This familiar refocusing of energies will open up development opportunities on real estate that had been locked up in federal government enclaves for decades. It is a part of a process that has been repeated dozens of times at communities throughout the United States over recent years.

But BRAC '05 was different than previous rounds. The real news in BRAC '05 was not with base closures but with major unit relocations around the nation. With the major global realignments proceeding as a part of this round of BRAC, there are sure to be many opportunities for development at major installations that are considered "gainers" in the restructuring. With major troop realignments throughout the country combined with some significant base closures, BRAC '05 may present some excellent commercial opportunities. But developers begin looking for opportunities now.

The "Peace Dividend"

The Department of Defense's (DOD) BRAC process is considered a necessary consequence of changing national security requirements following the Cold

War. The loosening of the Soviet Union's grip over Eastern Europe in the late 1980s marked the beginning of a new era for the U.S. military establishment. No longer faced with the likely threat of a direct battle against the Soviet Union in our global struggle against communism, the surge requirements of the U.S. military were considered reduced. Leaders in both political parties looked at the staggering costs of Cold War national defense as an opportunity to greatly reduce government spending.

The first round of base closures was approved in 1988, with subsequent BRAC rounds being approved in 1991, 1993, and 1995 under the authority of the Defense Base Closure and Realignment Act of 1990, which remains the basic "BRAC law," although it has been amended numerous times.[1] The latest round of BRAC was initially approved as a part of the DOD's spending authorization legislation for fiscal year 2002, and the military services made their recommendations for closures and realignments on May 13, 2005.[2] The Base Realignment and Closure Commission considered the DOD's recommendations and made its own recommendations on September 8, 2005, which were thereafter referred by the White House to Congress to become final.[3]

The BRAC law governs actions taken to close military installations where 300 civilian personnel are authorized to be employed, realignments at installations that create a reduction of more than 1,000 employees or by more than 50 percent of civilian personnel employed at an installation, and any construction or renovations resulting from those closures or realignments. Under the BRAC law, the military services are delegated the property disposal authority of the General Services Administration (GSA).[4] Also, the BRAC law exempts the BRAC commission's final recommendations from the requirements of National Environmental Policy Act (NEPA).[5] Thus, the services are not required to complete an environmental analysis of the decision whether to close or realign—rather their NEPA documents may focus on the effects of the actions that are within the services' discretion. For instance, in a realignment, a service would not focus on whether to move a unit to a particular installation but rather where on that installation to locate the unit's headquarters, housing, motor pools, and so forth. With respect to closures, the services must comply with NEPA during the process of property disposal.

Community Impact

To soften the economic blow of base closure, Congress in 1993 adopted the Base Closure Community Assistance Act, which calls upon the military services to work with communities to identify and implement means of reutilizing or redeveloping closing installations in such a way as to revitalize communities' economic prosperity.[6] In 1994, Congress approved legislation giving communities more flexibility in considering needs of the homeless in planning redevelopment, rather than imposing the strict homeless assistance requirements the federal government must follow under the McKinney Act of 1987.[7]

But closed installations do not automatically flow into the ownership of community developers. The military services are required to follow the GSA's federal property management regulations, which require that any excess federal property be screened by all other federal agencies to determine whether another agency has a need for the property. In previous rounds, a number of properties were snapped up by Department of the Interior (DOI) agencies, such as the U.S. Fish and Wildlife Service and the National Park Service. The military services, however, were often frustrated by the DOI's reluctance to take administrative control of property prior to completion of all environmental restoration activities. As a result, when the 2005 BRAC closure properties are screened, the military services will likely be insistent that any other federal agencies accept properties "as is." This should reduce the number or properties that are claimed in the federal property screening process.

Normally, base closure properties that are not claimed by other federal agencies will be taken by local redevelopment authorities, which are special purpose entities established by local governments for the sole purpose of managing the base closure properties. The local redevelopment authority (LRA) will be the community's primary development planner and point of contact with the military service that is disposing of an installation. To the extent possible, developers should be in contact with city local government officials as early as possible, perhaps even before an LRA is formed. The LRA is then responsible for preparing a redevelopment plan, which it will submit to the responsible military service. It will also work with the DOD's Office of Economic Adjustment to determine what economic assistance might be available to assist in developing the property for the community's best advantage.

Base closures, although they are typically dreaded for their impacts in local communities, are not always as devastating as the public believes. By freeing up significant federal land holdings for development, closed military installations may present significant economic opportunities. In an economically viable urban environment, opening land for development and getting it onto local tax rolls will sometimes far outweigh the economic detriment that resulted in a base's closure. Oakland Mayor Jerry Brown, for instance, used all of his political savvy in 2003 in getting the Oakland Army Base, which was located right in the city's commercial and industrial heart, transferred to the city's use as early as possible.

Property Transfer Issues

Under the Comprehensive Environmental Response, Compensation, and Liability Act (CERCLA), when a federal agency transfers ownership of cleaned-up property out of federal hands, it must normally include a deed provision that "covenants" that hazardous substances were present on the property and the nature of those hazardous substances, that those substances were cleaned up prior to transfer, and that the federal government will return to conduct any cleanup that is required to address any contamination that is discovered after transfer.[8] Thus, the basic premise of CERCLA calls for cleanup of contaminated federal property prior to its transfer into nonfederal hands. In 1996, Congress adopted the Community Environmental Response Facilitation Act (CERFA), amending CERCLA to spur the military services to identify clean properties at their BRAC installations that they could transfer quickly rather than waiting for the completion of the cleanup.[9] Under the CERFA amendments, the services are required to identify property on which "no hazardous substances and no petroleum products or their derivatives were known to have been released or disposed of" within 18 months after an installation is selected for closure or realignment.[10] Under the Act, the identification of a property as clean "is not complete until concurrence in the results is obtained, in the case of real property that is part of a facility on the National Priorities List, from the [Environmental Protection Agency (EPA)] Administrator, or, in the case of real property that is not part of a facility on the National Priorities List, from the appropriate State official."[11]

Congress has also authorized a special process for communities to obtain an "early transfer" of military base property.[12] Under an early transfer (or, as some say, "dirty transfer"), a federal agency can transfer land without completing all of its environmental restoration obligations required by CERCLA Section 120. Under "early transfer" authority, the federal government can transfer property without those "CERCLA covenants" as long as the governor of the state (or EPA Administrator in the case of a property on the National Priorities List) finds that the property transfer is protective of human health and the environment and that the government has made a showing that it will complete cleanup activities in satisfactory time.[13] When environmental cleanup is ultimately completed, the federal government must amend the deed to include the CERCLA covenants. Many DOD properties are sufficiently economically viable that communities are willing to accept them prior to completion of cleanup activities. Cleanup efforts are then completed either by the military service that is transferring the property or by the local redevelopment authorities, with the military service providing funding under the cooperative agreement authority of the Defense Environmental Restoration Program (DERP).[14]

There is also authority under the BRAC law itself for the services to transfer property to "any person who agrees to perform all environmental restoration, waste management, and environmental compliance activities that are required for the property or facilities under Federal and State laws, administrative decisions, agreements (including schedules and milestones), and concurrence."[15]

Land Use Controls and Residual Contamination

The requirement of many states to record use restrictions on contaminated properties provides an example of the type of conflict that can arise in conjunction with military land transfers. The quiet battle over federal and state prerogatives in environmental law compliance and enforcement, so evident throughout the military's interface with state regulators, has moved into the arena of real estate deals. Many states have adopted laws and regulations requiring recordation of restrictions in a real estate instrument as a condition on regulatory closure of environmental cleanup actions, a movement that has made federal managers uncomfortable in some states and adamantly defiant in others. California has chosen a moderate approach to applying the land use covenant requirement on federal property; nevertheless, the tension between state law and federal prerogatives has arisen in the details of applying the requirement.

A covenant to restrict the use of property is a mechanism recorded with a property deed under a California Department of Toxic Substances Control (DTSC) regulation that gives the State of California the ability to enforce land use and other environmental restrictions against property owners if an owner violates the covenant terms.[16] The requirement for the covenant applies when the environmental cleanup on a property will leave hazardous materials, hazardous wastes, or hazardous substances on the property at levels that are unsuitable for unrestricted use. Under the DTSC regulation, the department will not certify that an environmental response action has been completed if it leaves residual contamination in place until a covenant has been signed and recorded.[17]

With respect to federal property, under its regulation DTSC does not require the execution of the land use covenant as a part of an approved remedy but rather treats the covenant as a prerequisite to property transfer.[18] If it isn't feasible to record a land use covenant, such as when a federal agency proposes to transfer property to another federal agency, then the regulation allows the use of "other mechanisms to ensure that future land use will be compatible with the levels" of contamination left on the property, such as amending the federal facility's master plan.[19]

Land use controls provide a means by which a federal agency (or private entity) can accomplish a risk-based closure—conducting remedial action only to the extent necessary to allow reuse of the property for certain purposes with minimal risk. By putting use restrictions on a property, normally in the deed of conveyance, the federal agencies aim to ensure that the property will never be used for purposes inconsistent with the restrictions. To effectively protect human health and the environment, the use restrictions must be binding on both current and future landowners. Federal agencies may place use restrictions on a property to ensure the integrity of engineered structures (such as a cap) used as part of a cleanup remedy or to prevent potential human access to residual contamination. The U.S. Environmental Protection Agency has recognized the approach of placing land use restrictions on properties as an acceptable part of an environmental remedy. Because of questions raised recently over the effectiveness of the deed for enforcing the land use restrictions, however, states have begun adopting legislation requiring execution of a separate recordable document, granting a specific right to state regulatory agencies to enforce the restrictions in the instrument. California adopted such a requirement in 2003. Other states, such as Kentucky, Maryland, Nebraska, Ohio, South Dakota, Nevada, Maine, and West Virginia, have adopted the Uniform Environmental Covenants Act (UECA) for the same purpose.[20]

While California's land use covenant provision allows for exceptions to the covenant requirement at actively held federal property, Colorado has taken a much more aggressive approach, leading federal agencies and state regulators to loggerheads. Colorado's land use control recording requirement, adopted in 2001, gave the Colorado Department of Public Health and Environment (CDPHE) the authority to require land owners to record an "environmental covenant" as a mechanism for enforcing use restrictions established in conjunction with environmental cleanup actions that leave contamination in place.[21] The environmental covenants establish use restrictions, known as "institutional controls," that were relied on in making cleanup decisions. Such restrictions could include industrial use restrictions, dig restrictions, and the like. The Colorado law and implementing regulations make no distinction between federal and private property.[22] Federal agency representatives argued during the debate over the legislation that states lack the authority to require federal agencies to grant the environmental covenants on active federal property. Disputes over the requirement at both active military installations and base realignment and closure properties have brought the conflict to the fore in Colorado.

The federal agencies' argument against imposing the environmental covenant requirement on active installations is rooted on two principles—sovereign immunity and the property clauses of the U.S. Constitution. Under sovereign immunity, as we've discussed previously, only Congress can waive the federal government's immunity to lawsuits. States may regulate activities of federal agencies only when authorized to do so by Congress, and that authorization must be "clear and unambiguous." However, each of the major environmental statutes provides a limited waiver of sovereign immunity that requires federal facilities to comply with state laws. Normally, federal and state regulators have broad power to enforce pollution control requirements, such as the environmental covenant requirement. If a federal facility runs afoul of any of the numerous pollution standards, then the regulators have several civil remedies at their disposal, including injunctive relief.

As we've seen, however, the U.S. Supreme Court will not consider that Congress has waived sovereign immunity for enforcement purposes unless such a waiver has been "clear and unambiguous." The "clear and unambiguous" requirement was applied in considering the Clean Water Act and old Resource Conservation and Recovery Act (RCRA) federal facilities provisions in *Department of Energy v. Ohio*,[23] in which the Court determined that the Department of Energy could not be fined for past violations of the statutes. The Supreme Court showed that it could be surprisingly narrow in interpreting what constitutes a "clear and unambiguous" waiver.

Applying the "clear and unambiguous" standard for construing statutes, the federal agencies have argued that the current (post–Federal Facilities Compliance Act [FFCA]) RCRA waiver does not clearly waive sovereign immunity to the extent that it would allow a state to force the federal government to surrender a property interest. The waiver surrenders immunity from requirements "respecting control and abatement of . . . solid waste or hazardous waste disposal and management."[24] The federal agencies have contended that the waiver does not clearly and unambiguously allow for states to require a cession of property rights. The Colorado Attorney General's Office, by contrast, has argued that the waiver language is broad enough to encompass the environmental covenant requirement, which is a part of the state's regime for "control and abatement of solid waste or hazardous waste disposal and management."[25]

The constitutional argument is perhaps the stronger of the arguments advanced by the federal government. Under Article I, Section 8, clause 17, the U.S. Constitution reserved to Congress the power to "exercise exclusive Legislation in all Cases whatsoever, over . . . all Places purchased by the Consent of the Legislature of the State in which the Same shall be, for the Erection of Forts, Magazines, Arsenals, dock-Yards and other needful Buildings."[26] Further, under Article IV, Section 3, clause 2, "Congress shall have Power to dispose of and make all needful Rules and Regulations respecting the Territory or other Property belonging to the United States; and nothing in this Constitution shall be so construed as to

Prejudice any Claims of the United States, or of any particular State."[27] These provisions, the federal officials have argued, throw into question the notion that states would have jurisdiction over federally owned property.

But Daniel Miller of Colorado's Attorney General's Office has argued that the state's environmental covenant is not a property interest under Colorado law, despite the declaration in the legislation, that the covenant "shall run with the land and shall bind the owner of the land, the owner's successors and assigns, and any person using the land"[28] and that it "shall be recorded as any other instrument affecting title to and interests in real property."[29] In a journal article, he argued that a Colorado case, *Thornton v. Schobe*,[30] held that a common-law covenant restricting the use of law is not an interest in property.[31] He asserted that Colorado's interpretation should apply, under the Supreme Court's reasoning in *Reconstruction Fin. Corp. v. Beaver County*,[32] because it does not discriminate against the federal government nor run counter to the terms of federal law.[33]

Complicating matters is the fact that the services do not believe they have the authority to encumber actively held property. GSA has issued a memorandum stating that landholding agencies, including the military services, do not "have the authority to place such restrictions on property in their inventory." Citing the Federal Property and Administrative Services Act of 1949[34] as its authority, GSA stated that that it "views such restrictive covenants as disposals of real property . . . [and] GSA was given the exclusive authority to manage the utilization and disposal of property.[35] Further, as a matter of policy GSA frowns on environmental covenants on active federal property. "GSA is particularly concerned about requests to restrict the future use of property when the landholding agency does not contemplate declaring the property excess in the near future," the agency's policy memorandum stated. "GSA is doubtful as to the necessity, desirability or legal enforceability of placing restrictions on property that will remain in the Government's inventory. Questions as to how such restrictions will be enforced, and by whom, while the property is still an active Government facility are raised by these requests," the memorandum continued. "Further, it would be difficult, if not impossible, for GSA to accurately determine the impact such restrictions may have on the future disposal of the property when immediate disposal of the property is not being contemplated." The GSA memorandum concluded, "Therefore, GSA will deny all requests for land use restrictions on fully utilized property unless the requesting landholding agency can demonstrate the unique and extreme circumstances which would overcome GSA's objections to the placing of such restrictions on the property."[36]

Arguably, the conflict between Colorado and the federal government has been unnecessary given the purpose of the covenant requirement. As California recognized in implementing its land use covenant provision, the ultimate purpose is to ensure that the restrictions are observed so that human health and the environment are protected. The federal government has mechanisms in place to ensure that restrictions are observed for so long as the federal government owns a piece of property. It is when that property is transferred into the private sector that the risk of violation of restrictions—or of simply losing track of restrictions over time—is at its highest. By requiring federal agencies to impose the covenant at the time of transfer, California's DTSC has focused its energies more directly on the problem.

Land Use Covenant Issues in California

The federal government, and in particular the military services, generally view the California approach to land use covenants as a benefit because it allows the services to enlist the state to enforce the terms of specific restrictions imposed as part of their remedy under CERCLA. However, federal agency attorneys have found that they need to be mindful of the specific wording of the covenants, especially in light of the agencies' contentions in states such as Colorado that look to impose the requirement on active federal installations.

The Army's experience with land use covenants at base realignment and closure properties is instructive. Since California land use covenants are not intended to provide the state with the ability to enforce restrictions against the federal government at an active federal facility, the Army adopted a practice of drafting the covenants for properties pending transfer of ownership in such a way that they were not enforceable against the Army as either the "covenantor" or as the "current owner." As a result, the enforceable interest in the covenant would not take effect until after the Army had transferred a property into private hands.[37]

Under the Army's approach, land use covenants referenced specific use restrictions imposed as a part of the Army's remedy in its CERCLA record of decision (ROD). Those restrictions could include such controls as groundwater use or drinking restrictions, nondisturbance of protective caps, and so forth. As part of the covenant, a transferee would be required to notify DTSC of any potential violations of the covenant terms, including the use restrictions. In the Army's view, all parties—transferees, federal and state regulators, local government representatives, and the Army—should work together to ensure that land use restrictions are observed.

With respect to timing, the Army urged adoption of the covenant as close as possible to the effective date of the property conveyance. Optimally, the covenant terms would come into effect concurrent with the conveyance, leaving virtually no time before closing during which an executed, recorded covenant would apply to any preconveyance parcel. In the view of Army attorneys, signing a covenant long before transfer could create the impression that the Army was granting an enforceable interest to the state on active federal property. The Army did believe it has the authority to encumber actively held federal property, which is the responsibility of GSA.

The Army also continued to include all land use restrictions in deed provisions to ensure that it had a continued stake in ensuring compliance with restrictions. This alleviated the concern that, should DTSC fail to enforce a covenant, the Army would have some ability to enforce the same restrictions. In addition, all powers the Army desired to retain, such as the ability to disapprove a proposed modification of land use restrictions, were included in the deed as well.

The costs of overseeing the land use covenant requirements became an issue in Army property conveyances as well. Beginning in 2004, DTSC began requesting language in the covenants that would commit landowners to paying DTSC for oversight costs. The implementing regulation specified that DTSC "shall require responsible parties, facility owners or operators, or project proponents involved in land use covenants to pay all costs associated with the administration of such controls."[38] Typically, such oversight costs would include reviewing period compliance inspection reports submitted by landowners. While the regulation requires DTSC to extract payment, it didn't provide a specific authority to simply charge fees for reviewing compliance reports or other oversight. Thus, under a heading for "Costs of Administering this Covenant," DTSC officials wanted language to be included in the covenants to the effect that DTSC "has incurred and will in the future incur costs associated with the administration of this Covenant." The clause continued, "Therefore, the Owner hereby covenants for itself and for all subsequent owners that, pursuant to CCR Title 22, section 67391.1(h), the property owner agrees to pay the Department's costs associated with the administration of this Covenant." And, the clause continued, if "property ownership changes between the time [DTSC] incurs administrative costs and the invoice for such costs is received, each owner of the property for the period covered by the invoice as well as the current owner is responsible for such costs."

The Army and the other services basically saw two problems with proposed language. First, federal real estate attorneys questioned the validity of a clause in a real estate instrument under which one landowner would bind a subsequent landowner to pay money to a third party. Needless to say, property transferees objected to the language, since they had negotiated the real estate transaction without knowledge that such charges would be imposed and were learning of it at the tail end of the transaction. Whether such a provision would be binding under property law provisions or not, the Army and the other armed services viewed it as bad policy.

The second objection the Army and other armed services raised was that, since the "current owner" referred to in the last sentence of the clause was defined to include the federal government, by signing the covenant the federal agency would be signing up for a potential obligation to pay without a specific appropriation authorizing it, in violation of federal government spending laws. Under appropriations law principles, even a very remote potential to have to pay an obligation can be construed as a violation if it is not specifically authorized.

The Army and other armed services have objected to adopting the DTSC-drafted cost-recovery language in their covenants. As an approach to the future adoption of covenants, the Army has suggested to DTSC that oversight costs should be considered early on in negotiations by the parties to the federal real estate transaction, with the transferees agreeing to take on costs of ownership incident to ownership. This is consistent with the Army's overall land use restriction approach, which views observance of and compliance with use restrictions as a responsibility incident to property ownership. This agreement by the transferee to pay oversight costs to DTSC is not required to be contained in the covenant itself, and it is preferable to the Army to keep it out of that document because it is irrelevant to the direct purpose of establishing environmental use restrictions and a right in a third party regulator to enforce those use restrictions. The Air Force has adopted a similar approach of incorporating responsibility for oversight costs into the real estate transaction in an instrument other than the covenant itself. DTSC officials have thus far proven to be flexible in discussions regarding the collections of costs of oversight.

Environmental land use covenants have great potential to assist landowners to get contaminated land back into productive use so long as that use is consistent with safe use in light of residual contamination. Many states, including California, have recognized the notion of land use restrictions as a part of a cleanup remedy and have adopted means for executing covenants to ensure their enforceability. Since this is a fairly new area of environmental and real estate law, however, some issues could be expected to arise in implementing the covenant requirement, especially with regard to federal facilities. In their limited experience, the California regulators have proven to be responsible and flexible in their implementation of the covenant requirement. DTSC officials have recognized that imposing the land use covenant requirement on active federal property is unnecessary because other means are available to ensure that land use restrictions are followed. Despite a few minor conflicts, California regulators have kept the emphasis where it belongs—on the ultimate protection of human health and the environment. This flexibility and reasonableness in approach should ensure that former federal properties in California are held to a compliance standard at least as high as any other state.

Encroachment at Naval Air Station Oceana

After the DOD services submitted their recommendations for closure and realignment in May 2005, the BRAC Commission considered the recommendations at numerous hearings during the summer of 2005. Normally, such hearings focus on the specific installations named by the services. In 2005, however, the BRAC Commission looked beyond the Navy's recommendations to initiate a discussion on an installation the Navy had not recommended for closure—Naval Air Station Oceana in Virginia Beach, Virginia. The reason the commission insisted that Oceana should be considered for closure was because of "significant residential and commercial encroachment" surrounding the Oceana and its subinstallation, Naval Auxiliary Landing Fields Fentress, that had continued to inhibit low level flying and other training activities in the vicinity of the installation.[39] Beckoning the commission was the city of Jacksonville, Florida, which argued that the former Cecil Field, a victim of an earlier BRAC round, was prepared to accept relocation of the Navy's Atlantic Fleet Master Jet Base. After days of testimony, however, the commission determined that Oceana could remain open for the time being—but only if certain conditions were met. Among the conditions placed on the State of Virginia and the local community were enactment of legislation to prevent further encroachment at the facility, a plan to condemn and purchase incompatible use property located within likely accident zones and to spend no less than $15 million per year on obtaining the properties, and to consider rezoning within compatible use zones surrounding the installations.[40] While the BRAC Commission did ultimately vote to keep Oceana open, its considering the installation for closure highlighted the military's growing concern that development outside the gates of the military facilities should not hinder the training that takes place within or around the facilities—that consideration of the greater good should not be skewed against the national defense because of the environmental conditions surrounding a facility.

BRAC '05: A Departure from Prior BRAC Rounds

Much of the publicity leading up to the BRAC 2005 decisions surrounded DOD officials' predictions that this BRAC round would be larger than all previous BRAC rounds combined—that up to 20 percent of the military's infrastructure would be closed. Because of the global shifting of military assets, however, those early predictions have not proven correct. While the 2005 BRAC round is still larger than any single previous BRAC round with respect to closures, the real story in BRAC '05 is the drastic shift in troop strength from overseas back to the United States that has turned BRAC '05 into what Defense Department officials have referred to as a "Big R, little c" BRAC round.

The Army is at the heart of the change. As a part of BRAC '05, the Army plans to move some 15,000 troops from Germany to several stateside installations. Fort Bliss, Texas, is set to be the big winner in BRAC '05 with a net gain of 11,354 active duty soldiers, doubling its active duty population. Because of the realignments, Fort Bliss, already home to a family housing project of more than 3,200 units, could be expected to be the center of substantial private housing development in future years. In addition to Fort Bliss, Fort Benning, Georgia, expects to add 9,221 troops; Fort Carson, Colorado, will likely gain some 4,178 troops; Fort Sill, Oklahoma, will gain some 3,444 troops; and Fort Riley, Kansas, will grow by 2,415 soldiers.[41] Most of these realignments will be accomplished on an aggressive time schedule, permitting the entire realignment package to be accomplished as soon as possible. Some of the moves are dependent on other moves being completed first. The air defense artillery units at Fort Bliss, for instance, will have to move Fort Sill expeditiously to make room for units returning from Germany. Major facilities and infrastructure improvements will likely be required at each of the gaining installations to accommodate new troops, equipment, and command and control. The ability of construction contractors to mobilize rapidly to address the Army's needs will be a major advantage.

In addition to the troop shifts resulting in the Army's homeward move, a number of other installations are expected to grow substantially as the result of other BRAC-related decisions, such as the consolidation of medical training and command and control at Fort Sam Houston, Texas, which by DOD estimates was expected to grow by 7,648 soldiers and 1,624 civilians. For Aberdeen Proving Ground, Maryland, final numbers will be affected somewhat by the BRAC Commission's actions, but consolidation of some of the Army's research and development activities there was expected to increase the number of personnel by 2,176. In addition, the reduction in use of leased office space in northern Virginia is expected to shift about 12,000 jobs to Fort Belvoir, Virginia, and 5,000 jobs to Fort Meade, Maryland. In addition to the Army's major shifts, potential big gainers for the other services include Little Rock Air Force Base, with up to 3,898 new positions; Eglin Air Force Base, Florida, which expects 2,218 new personnel; Marine Corps Base Quantico,

Virginia, which expects to add 3,000 new personnel; and the Naval Air Weapons Station, China Lake, California, which may increase by 2,469 personnel.[42] All of these realignments will drive a need for new infrastructure and facilities that will vary from site to site. A major need at Fort Belvoir, for instance, will be for office space to accommodate the administrative functions that will move there as leased space is vacated in Arlington and Alexandria, Virginia. But any of these major shifts in personnel could present opportunities for development under currently existing authority or under creative future legislation. Because the timetables for establishing new facilities and infrastructure will be extremely aggressive, however, commercial developers should be exploring creative means to meet major military construction requirements at the earliest possible time.

Notes

1. Defense Base Closure and Realignment Act of 1990, Pub. L. 101-510 (codified at 10 U.S.C. § 2687 note).
2. Department of Defense, Base Closure and Realignment Report, vol. I (May 13, 2005).
3. Base Realignment and Closure Commission, 2005 Defense Base Closure and Realignment Commission Report, vol. I (Sept. 8, 2005).
4. 10 U.S.C. § 2687 note.
5. *Id.*; Defense Base Closure and Realignment Act, § 2905(c).
6. Base Closure Community Assistance Act, Pub. L. 103-160, Title 24, Subtitle A; National Defense Authorization Act for Fiscal Year 1994 (amending the Defense Base Closure and Realignment Act of 1990).
7. Base Closure Community Redevelopment and Homeless Assistance Act of 1994, Pub. L. 103-421 (amending Section 2905(b) of the *Defense Base Closure and Realignment Act of 1990*).
8. 42 U.S.C. § 9620(h)(3).
9. Community Environmental Response Facilitation Act, Pub. L. 102-426 (1996) (amending 42 U.S.C. § 9620[h]).
10. 42 U.S.C. § 9620(h)(4)(C).
11. *Id.* § 9620(h)(4)(B).
12. *Id.* § 9620(h)(3)(C).
13. *Id.*
14. 10 U.S.C. § 2701(d)(4).
15. Defense Base Closure and Realignment Act, § 2905(e).
16. Calif. Code Regs. tit. 22, § 67391.1.
17. *Id.*
18. *Id.* § 67391.1(e).
19. *Id.*

20. The National Conference of Commissioners on Uniform State Laws, *Uniform Environmental Covenants Act*, www.environmentalcovenants.org/ueca/UECAnews/UECAnews.htm (accessed Oct. 27, 2005).

21. Senate Bill 01-145 (SB145); COLO. REV. STAT. § 25-15-101 et seq.

22. *Id.*

23. Department of Energy v. Ohio, 503 U.S. 607 (1992).

24. 42 U.S.C. § 6961.

25. See Daniel S. Miller, *Looking a Gift Horse in the Mouth: Federal Agency Opposition to State Institutional Control Laws*, 32 ELR 11115 (2002).

26. U.S. CONST. art I, § 8, cl. 17.

27. U.S. CONST. art. IV, § 3, cl. 2.

28. COLO. REV. STAT. § 25-15-318.

29. COLO. REV. STAT. § 321.

30. Thornton v. Schobe, 243 P. 617 (1925).

31. Miller, *Looking a Gift Horse in the Mouth*, supra note 25, at 11121.

32. Reconstruction Fin. Corp. v. Beaver County, 328 U.S. 204 (1946).

33. Miller, *Looking a Gift Horse in the Mouth*, supra note 25, at 11122.

34. 40 U.S.C. § 471 et seq.

35. Memorandum from John Q. Martin, director, General Services Administration, Redeployment Services Division, Subject: Restrictive Covenants on Non-Excess Property, Oct. 16, 1998.

36. *Id.*

37. This approach reflected the Army's position as of August 2005, when I was the senior environmental attorney for the Army's BRAC program.

38. CALIF. CODE REGS. tit 22, § 67391.1(h).

39. BASE REALIGNMENT AND CLOSURE COMMISSION, 2005 DEFENSE BASE CLOSURE at 107.

40. *Id.*

41. DEPARTMENT OF DEFENSE, BASE CLOSURE AND REALIGNMENT REPORT.

42. *Id.*

II

ACCESS TO ENVIRONMENTAL INFORMATION

7

The Case for Access

The tradition of easy and free public access to government-held information and, more specifically, environmental information in the United States is deeply rooted.[1] Traditionally, even information about environmental impacts at military facilities has been relatively easy to access. Recent concerns over national security, however, have hindered the ease of obtaining environmental information in the United States. Despite the international concern over security issues, there has been a general international trend toward the increased availability of environmental information. The United Kingdom, for instance, has made great strides in recent years and has surpassed the United States by providing increased access to some types of environmental information. This is a result of the common belief that governments must allow greater public access to environmental information, including environmental information about military activities—so long as the information does not impair national security. The notion that greater access to environmental information will result in better environmental conditions has become an item of faith among many environmental activists. Few would question the premise that access to environmental information, even with regard to military activities, is a necessary component of a successful environmental program. However, given recent trends toward increased secrecy in light of international threats to security, a number of persuasive arguments must be advanced to support the position that we should foster free access to environmental information, with reasonable exceptions for legitimate national security concerns.

Public Access for Its Own Sake

Dealing with environmental matters in an "open society" requires public access to environmental information, as well as public participation in environmental decisions.[2] The recent trend toward greater public access to environmental information is the result of a consensus among Western nations that an informed public plays an important role in environmental protection and enhancement.[3] This consensus results from assumptions that are both philosophical and pragmatic. For instance, in promoting public access to environmental information, the U.S. Congress considered it in the context of its pragmatic function of enforcement by the public, in addition to considering any role it might have regarding "environmental rights."

On a philosophical level, supporters of environmental reform profess a kind of environmental "right-to-know" as part of a "right-to-participate."[4] Environmental rights are "often related to the concept of instilling some form of legal identity in the environment."[5] The premise is that everyone has a right to information regarding the "unowned" environment.[6] "The general public has an interest in all elements of the environment, which competes with other interests, including industrial operations. Where there are such competing interests, access to information on the impacts of those interests allows decisions to be made taking into account all the relevant factors."[7]

International agreements, such as the World Charter for Nature,[8] reflect a growing consensus that this view is well founded. The United Nations General Assembly, under the World Charter for Nature, adopted a resolution that "all persons, in accordance with their national legislation, shall have the opportunity to participate, individually or with others, in the formulation of decisions of direct concern to their environment, and shall have access to means of redress when their environment has suffered damage or degradation."[9] These "right-to-know" or "right-to-participate" philosophies can perhaps be viewed as a natural continuation of the trend toward increased democratization across the globe, particularly in Western nations.

The adoption of the Declaration on Environment and Development, or "The Rio Declaration," at the 1992 United Nations Conference on Environment and Development in Rio de Janeiro, exemplified additional support of increased access to environmental information.[10] The declaration states that "environmental issues are best handled with the participation of all concerned citizens, at the relevant level. At the national level, each individual shall have appropriate access to information concerning the environment that is held by public authorities, including information on hazardous materials and activities in their communities, and the opportunity to participate in decision-making processes. States shall facilitate and encourage public awareness and participation by making information widely available."[11]

Sierra Club attorney Neil A. F. Popovic describes access to environmental information as a critical element for effective public participation in environmental decision making. He wrote, "Without such information, public participation in environmental decision-making would seldom advance beyond shots in the dark."[12] He further declared that a "government's reactive duty to produce information complements its proactive duty to disseminate information."[13] Government agencies have an affirmative duty to provide certain types of information to the public, even if the public has not sought the information.[14] This is especially true for information regarding the potential dangers of hazardous substances.[15] Such provisions "perform an indispensable educational role by letting people know what is happening in and to their environment, paving the way for the public to participate in related decision-making."[16]

The United States has generally subscribed to the notion that public information and participation are requirements for a representative democracy. The First Amendment to the U.S. Constitution, which establishes freedom of the press and speech, supports this line of thinking.[17] The First Amendment reflects the framers' belief that public participation in government is inherently positive.[18] Congress applied this principle more concretely to governmental information with the passage of the Freedom of Information Act of 1966 (FOIA).[19] The FOIA establishes a presumption that information should be available to the public unless specific, well-defined reasons exist to withhold it.[20]

Another provision reflecting the public's "right-to-know" is the Emergency Planning and Community Right-to-Know Act of 1986.[21] This Act regulates industries that handle significant amounts of hazardous materials by requiring individual companies to keep a list of those materials and to advertise that the list is available to the public.[22] It provides an example of legislation reflecting Congress' apparent belief that there is an intrinsic value to access to environmental information.

The values of public participation and open government also exist in other advanced nations such as the United Kingdom. For example, in 1989, the United Kingdom amended the Official Secrets Act of 1911[23] to curb its rather severe policy of avoiding the release of information to the public.[24] Another example of the belief in government openness is in the government white paper, *This Common Inheritance*.[25] The white paper emphasized the importance of public access to environmental information by asserting that "if people are given the facts, they are best placed to make their own consumer decisions and to exert pressure for change as consumers, investors, lobbyists and electors."[26] In his foreword to a subsequent white paper proposing greater access to government information, the chancellor of the Duchy of Lancaster pronounced that "openness is fundamental to the political health of a modern state."[27] The white paper itself furthers this sentiment and states that "unnecessary secrecy in government leads to arrogance in governance and defective decision-making. The perception of excessive secrecy has become a corrosive influence in the decline of public confidence in government. Moreover, the climate of public opinion has changed: people expect much greater openness and accountability from government than they used to."[28]

Public Access for Enforcement Purposes

In addition to the philosophical notion that public access to information and participation in environmental decisions is a matter of public right, it is also a pragmatic means to ensure that environmental problems are addressed. The United States' environmental regulatory regime includes numerous provisions for "citizen suits" to enforce various environmental statutes.[29] Citizen suit provisions allow individual citizens, or groups of citizens, to take private or public entities to court for violations of environmental law.[30] Citizen suits inherently require access to certain environmental information. An example is the citizen suit provision of the U.S. Clean Water Act.[31] It creates an integrated enforcement system by placing enforcement powers in the hands of citizens to supplement the powers of federal or state enforcement agencies.[32] The Clean Water Act citizen suit provision requires the citizen or citizen group to provide 60 days notice to the administrator of the U.S. Environmental Protection Agency (EPA), the state concerned, and the company alleged to be in violation of emissions limits.[33] The provision also provides citizens with a cause of action against the EPA administrator "where there is alleged a failure of the Administrator to perform any act or duty under this chapter which is not discretionary with the Administrator."[34] In addition to civil penalties under the provision, which would likely not apply in an action against a military department, citizen-plaintiffs can seek injunctive relief to force the administrator to perform an act or duty or to enforce an effluent limitation.[35]

By creating a private right of action for citizen-plaintiffs, Congress has empowered the public to play a positive role in the enforcement of pollution standards. Thus, citizens are "watchdogs" over federal and state regulators based on their ability to bring a suit to control or compel regulator action.[36] Citizens are also "private attorneys general" because they supplement the enforcement power of government when inadequate personnel, funding, or motivation result in a shortfall of governmental information.[37] Almost every major environmental statute has a citizen suit provision.[38] In some instances, courts have found a right for citizens to sue to guarantee enforcement, even where Congress has not explicitly created a citizen suit provision.[39]

Some environmentalists believe that recent U.S. court decisions have diminished the effectiveness of citizen suit enforcement. In *Gwaltney of Smithfield, Ltd., v. Chesapeake Bay Foundation, Inc.*,[40] the U.S. Supreme Court held that jurisdiction under the Clean Water Act for citizen suits against past permit violators does not attach unless the citizen-plaintiff makes a good faith allegation that continuing violations are likely.[41] Critics of the Court's decision argued that this ruling damaged the deterrent effect of a potential suit because potential defendants may not be penalized if they wait until notice of a lawsuit to install pollution control equipment.[42] The U.S. Supreme Court again reduced the enforcement potential of the citizen suit in 1992 with its decision in *Lujan v. Defenders of Wildlife*.[43] The Court held that the citizen suit provision of the Endangered Species Act[44] did not confer standing on its own, and therefore, citizen-plaintiffs still had to establish standing to sue under the provision.[45] Despite the setbacks in *Gwaltney* and *Lujan*, the citizen suit remains a powerful tool in the environmentalist's arsenal, which was Congress's intent in including citizen suits in its overall environmental enforcement scheme.[46]

The concept of access to environmental information as an enforcement tool is present in other Western democracies as well. Other countries also provide for private action against polluters in certain circumstances. The United Kingdom, for instance, also provides civil remedies for private rights of action that are independent of regulatory provisions.[47] Although the United Kingdom has not explicitly established a right of action under its environmental statutes, the United Kingdom's system of "residual powers" allows the public to take direct enforcement action.[48] Generally, private citizens have a constitutional right to prosecute statutory offenses. This constitutional right, however, has often been explicitly limited by environmental statutes.[49] This right has been successfully exploited under a number of environmental statutes, but such powers are often overlooked.[50] Nevertheless, for this type of enforcement to be effective, the public must have access to environmental data to proceed with a case.[51]

Making Public Access Meet the Challenges

There are convincing reasons, both philosophical and pragmatic, for providing free public access to environmental information. Now that there is a consensus that environmental information should be accessible within the United States, as well as worldwide,[52] greater challenge still exists: how to determine the best means for providing access and how, if at all, that access should be limited. A significant legal framework exists to support the public's right to know about its environment in the United States, even with respect to military activities. But with recent challenges brought on by national security concerns, it is increasingly important to carefully determine the parameters of access to environmental information pertaining to the U.S. military. So long as national security is not impaired, environmental information regarding military activities should be as accessible as possible.

The provision of information is not, of course, an end in itself: it is a means to an end. At a general level it may be said that increased opportunities for public access to environmental information are seen as underpinning the objective of encouraging people, including people within the military establishment, to take on their responsibilities of stewardship.[53]

Scholars have identified five pragmatic benefits derived from liberal access to environmental information.[54] The first benefit is that it will reassure the public and promote confidence in governmental and industrial action, also known as the "public reassurance" role.[55] This is based on the premise that secrecy fuels fear and that withdrawal of secrecy promotes public confidence.[56] The second benefit of stewardship is that it will inform consumer choice, both in the demand for and in the consumption of goods: "For example, labelling may encourage consumers to opt for 'green' products; and information about the causes and consequences of pollution may encourage consumers to limit their use of cars and to reduce waste" in the use of natural resources.[57] This is referred to as the "personal responsibility" role.[58] The third benefit, known as the "industry responsibility" role,[59] states that "increased public scrutiny should encourage industries to take environmental protection seriously."[60] The fourth benefit is that "the knowledge that activities will come under public scrutiny should act as a 'vital discipline' for environmental protection agencies."[61] This is known as the "agency accountability" role.[62] The final benefit of stewardship is that "it will enable members of the public to play a role in policy formulation and decision-making on environmental matters," also known as the "public participation" role.[63]

All five of those above principles represent important reasons for making environmental information with respect to the military accessible to the public. The first principle, "public reassurance," is vital because it prompts governments to establish a climate of openness, rather than secrecy. This is important because secrecy breeds distrust.[64] Public reassurance can be a key commodity in accomplishing both environmental and national security goals, particularly with regard to the military, which has had a history of environmental problems.

To encourage consumer choice, the "personal responsibility" principle is also an important role for environmental information. This principle could provide economic incentives for environmental protection, as product manufacturers have already discovered that advertising "green friendly" products can be a marketing tool.[65] In addition, negative environmental information about a product can either force it off the market or force it to change.[66] For example, "green marketers" in the United States who make false or exaggerated environmental claims can expect scrutiny from the U.S. Federal Trade Commission.[67] In recent years, major "fast food" restaurant chains in the United States were pressured to market their products differently.[68] Additionally, some products that were packaged in aerosol spray cans are now aerosol free.[69] With respect to the military, news about an installation's environmental record could affect its community support. At a time at which community support is necessary to continue to train at a location and to accomplish mission objectives, such community support may be critical. The situation faced at Naval Air Station Oceana during the BRAC Commission's 2005 hearings is instructive. Had the Navy's reputation as an environmentally responsible member of the Virginia Beach community been in question, the community's willingness to rally behind the installation might have been in question as well.

The third principle, increasing "industry responsibility," may be important because it forces industries to improve their practices over time.[70] For instance, the citizen suit enforcement provisions in the United States provide an excellent stimulus for industries to ensure environmental compliance.[71] If the industries do not comply with existing water permits, for instance, industry officials know that they may be subject to a citizen suit, even if government regulators have not shown concern.[72] In addition, environmental information about an industry's products and production can bring tremendous economic pressure to change a product or production method to be more environmentally sound.[73] Thus, industries have a built-in incentive to recognize their environmental responsibilities. With respect to the military services and to the military industrial complex, this pressure is just as firm as it is for private industry.

The "agency accountability" principle puts pressure on the environmental enforcement agencies that are charged with ensuring compliance with environmental law.[74] "Openness in government," agreed U.S. President Clinton, "is essential to accountability."[75] Government agencies are not always models of efficiency. Further, employees are sometimes outright lazy or corrupt. Public scrutiny may place pressure on environmental enforcement agencies to do their jobs and to do them well.[76] In addition, increased availability of information about agencies might have the added benefit of reinforcing public confidence in government actions.[77] If the public were to get the impression that environmental regulators were unduly favoring military facilities, the resultant pressure might compel such a regulator to give closer scrutiny to those military facilities.

Finally, the "public participation" principle currently plays an integral role in environmental law.[78] This role is both pragmatic and an important part of the more intangible "right-to-participate."[79] In the environmental decision-making process, members of the public may have relevant facts or information to contribute.[80] A lack of public access could create an information vacuum, which could hinder the availability of relevant information.[81] With regard to environmental investigations at military installations, such as a NEPA environmental study or an environmental survey to locate potential hazardous substance contamination, members of the local community might in some instances have more "institutional knowledge" about historical practices on base than the active duty personnel temporarily assigned there. As such, efforts to cooperate with the community can greatly enhance the thoroughness of such studies while at the same time raise public confidence in the environmental condition of the facilities—or by contrast make the public aware of hazards that should be avoided. Over the years, public awareness programs have greatly improved local communities' perceptions of environmental cleanup efforts at such environmentally controversial installations as the Army's Aberdeen Proving Ground, Maryland, where three employees were once convicted of RCRA violations in the late 1980s.

Notes

1. The tradition of freedom of access to public information was in place prior to passage of any of the modern environmental acts. See Laura Schenck, *Freedom of Information Statutes: The Unfulfilled Legacy*, 48 FED. COMM. L.J. 371–74 (1995).

2. Ludwig Krämer, *The Open Society, Its Lawyers and Its Environment*, 1 J. ENVTL. L. 1, 4 (1989). An "open society" is defined as a place where "governments derive their right to govern from the consent of the governed and where the setting of standards does not consist of transforming shadows of the Platonic idea of Justice into a piece of legislation, but are conceived, scheduled and accepted by way of democratic procedure."

3. See STUART BELL, BALL & BELL ON ENVIRONMENTAL LAW: THE LAW AND POLICY RELATING TO THE PROTECTION OF THE ENVIRONMENT, 4th ed., 161–62 (1997).

4. Neil A. F. Popovic, *The Right to Participate in Decisions That Affect the Environment*, 10 PACE ENVTL. L. REV. 683, 708 (1993) (stating that "public participation in environmental decision-making requires . . . ready access to government-controlled information" on the environment).

5. BELL, BALL & BELL ON ENVIRONMENTAL LAW, supra note 3, at 161.

6. *Id.*

7. *Id.*

8. G.A. Res. 37/7, UN GAOR, 37th Sess., Supp. No. 51, at 17, UN Doc. A/37/51 (1983).

9. *Id.* at 18 (referencing principle 23); Popovic, *The Right to Participate*, supra note 4, at 687.

10. Gumisai Mutume, *Finance: Corporations Merely Wrapping Themselves in U.N. Flag*, INTER PRESS SERVICE, July 21, 2000, LEXIS, World Library, Inpres File; United Nations Conference on Environment and Development, Adoption of Agreements on Environment and Development, Agenda item 21, at 7–17, UN Doc. A/Conf/151/5 (1992).

11. *Id.* at 3 (quoting principle 10).

12. Popovic, *The Right to Participate*, supra note 4, at 694.

13. *Id.* at 696.

14. *Id.* at 692–98; William J. Clinton, Memorandum on the Freedom of Information Act, 2 PUB. PAPERS 1685 (Oct. 4, 1993).

15. Popovic, *The Right to Participate*, supra note 4, at 697.

16. *Id.* at 696.

17. U.S. CONST. amend. I.

18. *Id.*

19. 5 U.S.C. § 552.

20. *Id.*

21. 42 U.S.C. §§ 11001–50.

22. *Id.* §§ 11021, 11023.

23. *Official Secrets Act of 1911*, 1 and 2 Geo. 5, ch. 28, § 2 (Eng.).

24. *Official Secrets Act of 1989*, ch. 6, § 2 (Eng.) (providing provisions that protect more limited classes of official information).

25. THIS COMMON INHERITANCE, Cm. 1200 (HMSO 1990).

26. *Id.* at 12.

27. The Chancellor of the Duchy of Lancaster, foreword, YOUR RIGHT TO KNOW: THE GOVERNMENT'S PROPOSALS FOR A FREEDOM OF INFORMATION ACT, Cm. 3818 (1997).

28. *Id.* at 1.

29. 33 U.S.C. § 1365(a); see also Middlesex County Sewerage Auth. V. Natl. Sea Clammers Assn., 453 U.S. 1, 14 (1981). The Middlesex court held that Congress preempted federal common law nuisance actions by passing pollution control legislation with defined remedies (21–22).

30. Harold Feld, *Saving the Citizen Suit: The Effect of Lujan v. Defenders of Wildlife and the Role of Citizen Suits in Environmental Enforcement*, 19 COLUM. J. ENVTL. L. 141, 143–45 (1994).

31. *Id.*, note 16, at 144; 33 U.S.C. § 1365.

32. See, e.g., Middlesex County Sewerage Auth., 453 U.S. at 14.

33. 33 U.S.C. § 1365(b)(1)(A). Actions by citizens are barred if the EPA or a state is already actively pursuing enforcement (§ 1365[b][1][B]).

34. *Id.* § 1365(1)(2).

35. *Id.* § 1365(a).

36. See 33 U.S.C. § 1365(a).

37. Feld, *Saving the Citizen Suit*, supra note 30, at 144.

38. Feld, *Saving the Citizen Suit*, supra note 30, at 144; see, e.g., 15 U.S.C. § 2619; 42 U.S.C. § 300j-8; 42 U.S.C. § 6972(a); 42 U.S.C. § 7604(a); 42 U.S.C. § 9659(a); 42 U.S.C. § 11046(a)(1).

39. See Sierra Club v. Morton, 405 U.S. 727, 731–34 (1972) (finding that citizens may invoke the judicial process without relying on specific statutory authorization, if they have a personal stake or interest in the outcome of the action).

40. See Gwaltney of Smithfield, Ltd., v. Chesapeake Bay Found., Inc., 108 S. Ct. 376 (1987).

41. *Gwaltney of Smithfield*, 108 S. Ct. at 386. The citizen suit provision of the Clean Water Act provides jurisdiction for suits when a permit holder is "alleged to be in violation" (33 U.S.C. § 1365[a][1]). The Court interpreted this to mean that the provision for citizen suits is prospective in orientation and that cases would become moot if, during the course of the litigation, a defendant could show that there was no continuing likelihood of violation (*Gwaltney of Smithfield*, 108 S. Ct. at 386). The Foundation argued that the phrase "to be in violation" should not be interpreted strictly and that "it would ill serve the framers of the law to ignore their intent because we were constrained to pretend they were always punctilious grammarians." (*Gwaltney of Smithfield*, 108 S. Ct. at 376 [No. 86-473], Brief for Respondents at 8).

42. William A. Wilcox Jr., *Environmental Law—Will Jurisdiction Attach in Citizen Suits against Wholly Past Permit Violators under Section 505 of the Clean Water Act, 33 U.S.C. section 1365?* 24 LAND & WATER L. REV. 153, 161 (1989). It is argued that this leaves government regulators as the only effective deterrent force against polluters, and if government regulators in a state or region are ineffective or inefficient, potential defendants have little to fear. See *id.* Although *Gwaltney* placed a greater burden on citizen-plaintiffs and foreclosed suits against permit violators when those violators are able to cure the cause of violations prior to suit, citizen suits nevertheless remain a powerful tool for citizens groups even after *Gwaltney.* See *id.* at 160. In fact, when *Gwaltney* itself was remanded to the district court, the judge found against the defendant again, on the basis of expert testimony that showed there was some likelihood of continuing violations during winter months. *Chesapeake Bay Found., Inc., v. Gwaltney of Smithfield, Ltd.*, 688 F. Supp. 1078, 1079 (E.D. Va. 1988).

43. Lujan v. Defenders of Wildlife, 504 U.S. 555 (1992).

44. 16 U.S.C. § 1540(g).

45. *Lujan*, 504 U.S. at 558–62. Prior to Lujan, a plaintiff, under authority of one of the citizen suit provisions, could simply establish standing by alleging a violation of the pertinent statute and asserting that it affected him in some way. Feld, *Saving the Citizen Suit*, supra note 30, at 141.

46. See Feld, *Saving the Citizen Suit*, supra note 30, at 144, 147, 182.

47. See BELL, BALL & BELL ON ENVIRONMENTAL LAW, supra note 3, at 151.

48. *Id.*

49. *Id.*

50. *Id*; see, e.g., *Water Industry Act*, c. 56, § 211 (1991) (Eng.).

51. BELL, BALL & BELL ON ENVIRONMENTAL LAW, supra note 3, at 151.

52. See, e.g., Popovic, *The Right to Participate*, supra note 4, at 687–88 (citing World Charter for Nature; the International Union for the Conservation of Nature and Natural Resources; and the Rio Declaration—all demanding access to information).

53. See Jeremy Rowan-Robinson et al., *Public Access to Environmental Information: A Means to What End?* 8 J. ENVTL. L. 19, 20 (1996).

54. *Id.*
55. *Id.*
56. *Id.*
57. *Id.*
58. *Id.*
59. *Id.*
60. *Id.*
61. *Id.* at 21.
62. *Id.*
63. *Id.*
64. See, e.g., Statement by the President upon Signing the "Freedom of Information Act," 316 PUB. PAPERS 699 (July 4, 1966).
65. See Mark Landler et al., *Suddenly, Green Marketers Are Seeing Red Flags*, BUS. WK., Feb. 25, 1991, at 74.
66. See Dennis E. Garrett, *The Effectiveness of Marketing Policy Boycotts: Environmental Opposition to Marketing*, J. MARKETING 46 (Apr. 1987) (discussing the effectiveness of such "environmental boycotts").
67. See Landler et al., *Suddenly*, supra note 65, at 74.
68. Garrett, *The Effectiveness of Marketing*, supra note 66, at 46.
69. See, generally, *id.*
70. See Rowan-Robinson et al., *Public Access to Environmental Information*, supra note 53, at 20.
71. See *id.*
72. 33 U.S.C. § 1365(a)(1).
73. See Garrett, *The Effectiveness of Marketing*, supra note 66, at 47.
74. See Rowan-Robinson et al., *Public Access to Environmental Information*, supra note 53, at 21.
75. Clinton, Memorandum, supra note 14, at 1685.
76. See Rowan-Robinson et al., *Public Access to Environmental Information*, supra note 53, at 21.
77. For example, Popovic identified enhancing public acceptance of public decisions and building consensus as functions of public participation. Popovic, *The Right to Participate*, supra note 4, at 685 (citing ADVISORY COMMISSION ON INTERGOVERNMENTAL RELATIONS, CITIZEN PARTICIPATION IN THE AMERICAN FEDERAL SYSTEM 30, 61–63 [1979]).
78. See Rowan-Robinson et al., *Public Access to Environmental Information*, supra note 53, at 21.
79. See Popovic, *The Right to Participate*, supra note 4, at 683, 684.
80. *Id.* at 685.
81. See William A. Tilleman, *Public Participation in the Environmental Impact Assessment Process: A Comparative Study of Impact Assessment in Canada, the United States and European Community*, 33 COLUM. J. TRANSNATL. L. 339, 343 (1995).

8

Environmental Information and the U.S. Military

WITH EXCEPTIONS FOR NATIONAL SECURITY CONSIDERATIONS, information about environmental impacts of military activities is generally available to the American public. This fact has contributed significantly to the public's awareness of the environmental effects of military activities and has arguably reduced the potential that the military services would receive preferential treatment from environmental regulators. "With increased use of the Freedom of Information Act to gain access to government records," wrote Professor Stephen Dycus, "and with the enactment of environmental laws that require monitoring and disclosure of federal facility activities, the public is better informed and less tolerant of many defense-related environmental injuries that earlier would have been dismissed, without question, as unavoidable."[1]

In the United States, there is no specific environmental information legislation like that adopted in European Community nations.[2] This is largely because there is no need. The environmental community, including environmental interest groups, makes liberal use of the Freedom of Information Act of 1966 (FOIA) to obtain federal environmental information from the federal government, including the Department of Defense and the Department of Energy, and state environmental information, which includes regulator information about military installations, from state agencies.[3]

Beyond the general requirements of the FOIA, however, the various environmental laws do address public awareness and participation values. Specific environmental statutes impose duties on governmental bodies to provide environmental information to the public that require more than simply answering FOIA requests.[4] Government agencies must maintain databases of information that are easily accessible to the public.[5] Under the environmental statute requirements, individual states must meet the record-keeping and public access requirements of the federal statutes and must be in compliance with federal environmental law.[6] Many of the major U.S. environmental statutes have their own industry reporting requirements, which by virtue of waivers of sovereign immunity also apply to the military services.[7] The laws themselves require holders of environmental permits to collect certain types of environmental information pertaining to monitoring compliance with, and identifying and enforcing violations of, environmental laws.[8] Permit holders must submit this information to the government for public disclosure.[9] Such records are maintained by state regulating offices and are accessible on demand by members of the public.[10] The Environmental Protection Agency (EPA), in turn, maintains a national database by compiling all the environmental data provided by the states.[11] Thus, significant amounts of information about the environmental performance of the military services can be obtained from third parties—the regulators—through the public databases that they maintain.

Under the Clean Water Act of 1977 (CWA), for instance, discharge monitoring reports and other information submitted to environmental regulators "shall be available to the public, except that upon a showing satisfactory to the Administrator by any person that . . . [the information] (other than effluent data) . . . if made public would divulge methods or processes entitled to protection as trade secrets of such person."[12] Thus, the burden of proof is on the person submitting the information to show that it constitutes a trade secret. Otherwise, under no circumstances may the public be denied the actual effluent data for a plant or facility.[13] National security is not given as a basis for an exemption from the public reporting requirements of the CWA, although the public reporting requirements would be encompassed by an overall compliance exemption from CWA requirements if the president determined it to be in "the paramount interest of the United States."[14] Much of the information on environmental quality in local communities is available on the EPA's website, which, according to the EPA, receives over forty million contacts from members of the public per month.[15]

In addition, most U.S. statutes require that the public be notified before environmental regulators take certain actions, such as granting or denying an environmental permit.[16] The Resource Conservation and Recovery Act of 1976 (RCRA), for instance, requires that notice of any proposed permit be published in a local newspaper of general circulation and, further, requires that the public be allowed to comment and attend a public hearing.[17] The requirement also applies when military and nonmilitary government agencies apply for a RCRA permit. Under such procedures, the public is more than a mere spectator. The EPA or state regulatory body must take into account the comments of the public in rendering its decision to grant or deny a permit.[18] Members of the public may also appeal initial decisions of the permitting authorities.[19] Under the CWA, for instance, any "interested person," including members of the public, may appeal the terms of a proposed permit under that statute's National Pollutant Discharge Elimination System.[20]

As a result of the constant reporting of environmental information under environmental statutes and the openness of permitting processes, the United States has a system that is available for public access and participation. Regarding property contamination (or "brown fields") cases, for instance, real estate lawyers have found that "much of the work to be done in establishing both liability and damages can be derived from public records."[21] By 1990, "In most cases [involving contaminated land], the information [was] available for inspection and copying with a telephone call or an over-the-counter request."[22] Information from government agencies can include such information as geology and groundwater hydrology for a locality; local groundwater conditions; existing site evaluation and spill reports for a specific property and nearby properties; chemical inventories of previous owners; environmental permits of present and previous landowners and compliance histories; and building use permits of previous owners or occupiers.[23] Information about environmental conditions at military installations is available on many of these databases.

The Emergency Planning and Community Right-to-Know Act

In addition to the information that environmental regulators are required to make available under individual environmental statutes, the U.S. government has also enacted broad "right-to-know" laws that require the disclosure of certain routine information not necessarily related to monitoring, enforcing, or obtaining permits.[24] The Emergency Planning and Community Right-to-Know Act of 1986 (EPCRA)[25] is at the forefront of this genre of legislation.[26] Government facilities, including military installations, are expected to comply with EPCRA's requirements and do so, even with respect to installations that have historically housed the U.S. chemical weapons stockpile.

Under EPCRA, facilities with significant quantities of "extremely hazardous substances" on site are required to notify local emergency planning officials (local emergency planning committees or LEPCs) and must designate a representative to participate in local emergency planning activities as an emergency response coordinator.[27] Facilities that have more than 10,000 pounds of any "hazardous chemical" on site must submit copies of material safety data sheets (MSDSs) for each chemical, or a listing of all MSDSs on site to the LEPC and to state emergency response officials (state emergency response commissions or SERCs).[28] Many large industrial facilities must also submit an annual inventory of hazardous chemicals.[29] Once this data is submitted to the LEPCs, the LEPCs must make available to the public both the data and the emergency response plans that are supposed to incorporate and address the potential hazards posed by the hazardous chemical data collected.[30] Under EPCRA, each LEPC "shall annually publish a notice in local newspapers that the emergency response plan, material safety data sheets, and inventory forms have been submitted . . . [and] that members of the public who wish to review any such plan, sheet, form, or followup notice may do so at the location designated."[31]

In addition to the routine planning requirements of EPCRA, a facility must report information about certain spills or releases to government authorities, which will be maintained as part of a register.[32] Such information must be reported if a facility (1) is involved in manufacturing; (2) employs more than ten workers; (3) manufactures or processes more than 25,000 pounds of the chemical or uses more than 10,000 pounds during the year; and (4) the chemical is listed among some 350 specific toxic chemicals or chemical categories.[33] The release forms "are intended to provide information to federal, state, and local governments and the public, including citizens of communities surrounding covered facilities."[34] Such information includes types and amounts of pollutants spilled or released, and results of emergency response efforts to clean up the spills or releases.[35] Each state must thereafter maintain a listing, known as the toxic release inventory (TRI), of all such statewide releases by locality.[36] According to the Commission for Environmental Cooperation, which reports on Canadian, Mexican, and U.S. environmental matters, some 65,000 industrial facilities nationwide are subject to TRI reporting.[37] As with other public information statutes in the United States, there are exemptions from TRI reporting.[38] Such exemptions include trade secret information, chemicals used in laboratories, or chemicals present in the structure of a facility or in an article of manufacture.[39]

Environmental Impact Assessment

As discussed previously, the main environmental planning statute in the United States, and arguably the most significant of all environmental statutes, is the National Environmental Policy Act (NEPA), which dates back to 1969.[40] Among the goals of NEPA is to "encourage and facilitate public involvement in decisions which affect the quality of the human environment."[41]

The implementing regulations for NEPA, which were developed by the Council on Environmental Quality (CEQ), establish an intricate set of rules for conducting the type of environmental analysis that is required for a given action or project.[42] Federal agencies, including the military services, have further elaborated on those requirements in their own regulations.[43] Consistent with the public participation goal of NEPA, public consultation is an important part of the NEPA process. At the very beginning of the environmental impact statement (EIS) process, for instance, notice must be given to all other agencies and concerned individuals about the proposal.[44] This is done through an announcement in the Federal Register and followed up with more specifically targeted invitations to agencies and individuals, including project opponents.[45] After the public is invited to participate in "scoping" procedures by providing its input on the nature of the proposed action or activity,[46] the EIS will go through two stages.[47] First, the agency releases a public draft on which the public may comment about the environmental consequences of the proposal.[48] In issuing a final EIS, the agency must "assess and consider comments both individually and collectively."[49] The agency, however, is not required to change its plans because of the public comment, but it would have that option if changes were warranted.

The CEQ regulations require a high degree of public involvement. Agencies must, for instance, "make diligent efforts to involve the public in preparing and implementing their NEPA procedures."[50] Agencies must also "provide public notice of NEPA-related hearings, public meetings, and the availability of environmental documents so as to inform those persons and agencies who may be interested or affected."[51] Thus, agencies must make public the notice of availability of an environmental assessment (EA), even when the agency determines that there would be no significant impact to the environment.[52] Agencies must also sponsor or hold public hearings "whenever appropriate or in accordance with statutory requirements applicable to the agency."[53]

NEPA does not apply to the private sector.[54] It does not apply to separate states either, although at least twenty-seven states now have environmental impact assessment programs for analyzing state projects.[55] Some states hold more faithfully to NEPA than others.[56] Although NEPA does not apply to states and private entities, it does apply when some federal decision making is involved, such as the granting of a lease, license, or right-of-way, or allowing the issuance of a permit under one of the environmental statutes.[57] For example, constructing a dock or pier adjacent to a river or a lake would require a permit from the U.S. Army Corps of Engineers to be in compliance with the Rivers and Harbors Act of 1910.[58] The corps would require that an EIS be done prior to making its permit decision.[59] Additionally, projects that include some portion of the project on federal land, such as a long-distance pipeline, would require NEPA documentation, because location of the federal pipeline on federal property would require a federal decision, "which may have an impact on man's environment."[60]

While the European Community Directive on environmental assessment excludes national defense activities from its application, the United States' NEPA does not.[61] NEPA does, however, make public disclosure of NEPA documents subordinate to the public release rules of the FOIA.[62] While NEPA documentation for classified military projects can be kept secret, the environmental assessment must still be performed. That documentation is subject to in camera review, as provided by the FOIA.[63] While some national defense environmental assessment information can be denied to the public under NEPA, the statute does not provide a blanket exemption.[64] In the alternative, a federal agency in an emergency situation can seek to apply the alternative procedures policy allowed for under the CEQ regulations.[65] The alternative procedures, however, are not intended to excuse the agency completely from its NEPA analysis responsibility.

Notes

1. Stephen Dycus, National Defense and the Environment 1 (1996).

2. See, e.g., Environmental Information Regulations, S.I. 1992/3240 (1992) (Eng.).

3. 5 U.S.C. § 552.

4. N. Am. Commn. for Envtl. Cooperation, Summary of Environmental Law in North America, § 5.1 (1995).

5. See *id.* § 5.2 (discussing the requirements for the reporting of environmental information for industry).

6. See *id.*; see, e.g., 42 U.S.C. §§ 7414(b), 7543; 33 U.S.C. § 1318 (c).

7. For examples of such requirements, see 42 U.S.C. §§ 7414, 7542, 7651(k), 7671(b); 33 U.S.C. § 1318; and 42 U.S.C. 9604(b). It should be also noted that 5 U.S.C. §§ 551–59, 701–06, gives the public an opportunity to participate in the federal agency rule-making process (§ 553). Therefore, the public has an opportunity to comment or contest any regulation a federal environmental regulator might adopt prior to its adoption.

8. 42 U.S.C. §§ 7414, 7542, 7651(k), 7671(b); 33 U.S.C. § 1318; 42 U.S.C. § 9604(b).

9. 33 U.S.C. § 1318 (a); Deirdre H. Robbins, *Doing Business in the Sunshine: Public Access to Environmental Information in the United States*, 3 Rev. of Eur. Community & Intl. Envtl. L. 26, 29 (1994).

10. 33 U.S.C. § 1318(b); Robbins, *Doing Business in the Sunshine*, supra note 9, at 29. Many such records are available electronically through the Internet. A simple computer search can now reveal, for instance, the names of every Clean Water Act permit holder in a locality and its compliance status.

11. This database may be accessed at EPA regional libraries or via the EPA website at www.epa.gov.

12. 33 U.S.C. § 1318(b)(2).

13. *Id.*
14. 33 U.S.C. § 1323(a).
15. The EPA maintains its Internet site at www.epa.gov. By accessing this site, members of the public may call up useful environmental information from throughout the United States or link to state databases.
16. See, e.g., 42 U.S.C. § 6974(b).
17. *Id.*
18. *Id.*
19. See, e.g., 40 C.F.R. § 124.74.
20. 33 U.S.C. § 1319(g)(4).
21. Robert C. Thompson, *Public Records in Property Contamination Cases*, PRAC. REAL EST. LAW. 77 (Nov. 1990). Real estate lawyers are particularly interested in accessing information on contaminated properties because of strict joint and several liability imposed by the Comprehensive Environmental Response, Compensation, and Liability Act (CERCLA), under which an unwitting landowner who has contributed nothing to contamination at a site may be held responsible for the contamination caused by previous owners (78–79).
22. *Id.* at 78.
23. *Id.* at 79–82.
24. N. AM. COMMN., SUMMARY, supra note 4, § 5.52.
25. 42 U.S.C. §§ 11001–50.
26. *Id.* EPCRA is also known as Title III of the Superfund Amendment and Reauthorization Act of 1986 (SARA) because of its codification within the code sections applying to what is commonly known as the "Superfund Act of 1980" (see §§ 11046, 9607).
27. 40 C.F.R. § 355.30.
28. *Id.* §§ 355.20–355.25.
29. *Id.* §§ 370.20(d), 370.25.
30. 42 U.S.C. § 11044.
31. *Id.* § 11044(b).
32. *Id.* §§ 11023(a), 11023(h).
33. *Id.* §§ 11023(b)(1)(A), 11023(c), 11023(f).
34. *Id.* § 11023(h).
35. *Id.* § 11023(g).
36. *Id.* §§ 11023(h), 11044(a).
37. N. AM. COMMN., SUMMARY, supra note 4, at § 5.2.
38. See 42 U.S.C. §§ 11023, 11042.
39. See *id.*
40. *Id.* §§ 4321–70(a).
41. 40 C.F.R. § 1500.2(d).
42. *Id.* §§ 1500–1508.
43. See, e.g., 32 C.F.R. §§ 651.8, 651.28 (replacing ARMY REG. 200-2, ENVIRONMENTAL EFFECTS OF ARMY ACTIONS, Dec. 23, 1988).
44. *Id.* § 1501.7.
45. *Id.*

46. *Id.* §1501.7.
47. *Id.* §§ 1503.1(a)(4), 1503.4(a).
48. *Id.* § 1503.1(a)(4).
49. *Id.* § 1503.4(a).
50. *Id.* § 1506.6(a).
51. *Id.* § 1506.6(b).
52. See *id.* §§ 1506.6(b), 1508.13.
53. *Id.* § 1506.6(c).
54. See *id.* § 1500.1(a) (indicating that NEPA involves federal agencies); William A. Tilleman, *Public Participation in the Environmental Impact Assessment Process: A Comparative Study of Impact Assessment in Canada, the United States and European Community*, 33 COLUM. J. TRANSNATL. L. 339, 372 (1995) (noting that NEPA applies to "federal actions").
55. Tilleman, *Public Participation*, supra note 54, at 365.
56. *Id.* at 365–66.
57. *Id.* at 372–73.
58. *Id.* at 372.
59. *Id.*
60. *Id.*
61. *Id.* § 4332(2)(C).
62. *Id.*
63. 5 U.S.C. § 552(a)(4)(B).
64. 42 U.S.C. § 4332(2)(C).
65. 40 C.F.R. § 1506.11.

9

Freedom of Information in the United States

When U.S. President Lyndon B. Johnson signed the Freedom of Information Act (FOIA) into law on July 4, 1966 ("Independence Day"), none of the bill's sponsors were invited to witness the signing.[1] They had not been informed that the bill would be signed, and despite the urging of White House staffers and members of Congress, there was no bill-signing ceremony.[2] Nevertheless, Johnson's unceremonious signing[3] of the bill culminated more than a decade of efforts to pass the FOIA.[4]

Despite the vision of early Americans such as James Madison, Thomas Jefferson, and Patrick Henry that "a strong democracy depended on an informed electorate,"[5] the level of free access that Americans now have over government information was many years in the making. The Administrative Procedure Act of 1946 (APA),[6] in its original form, had attempted, unsuccessfully, to provide easy access to government information. The APA, however, contained language that provided wide discretion to agencies to withhold records if the requester was not "directly or properly concerned," or if the agency determined to keep the records confidential "for good cause shown."[7] In 1958, Congress amended a 1789 "housekeeping" statute that gave federal agencies the authority to keep records.[8] That statute had been used as authority for withholding records, so Congress added the following restriction: "This section does not authorize withholding information from the public or limiting the availability of records to the public."[9]

Eventually, Congress acted to provide clear, comprehensive guidance on disclosure of information within the APA by passing the FOIA in 1966, which amended Section 3 of the APA.[10] The FOIA provided clear guidance in establishing a presumption in favor of disclosure of government information and replaced the vague "for good cause shown" premise for denying disclosure with a detailed list of exemptions.[11] It covered the whole executive branch of the federal government, including agencies that held records pertaining to the environment.[12]

When President Johnson signed the FOIA, his accompanying statement declared that he did so "with a deep sense of pride that the United States is an open society in which the people's right to know is cherished and guarded."[13] Johnson's statement reflected the belief that freedom of information should only be limited in compelling circumstances.[14] "This legislation springs from one of our most essential principles: A democracy works best when the people have all the information that the security of the Nation permits. No one should be able to pull curtains of secrecy around decisions which can be revealed without injury to the public interest."[15] Johnson further added that he had "always believed that freedom of information is so vital that only the national security, not the desire of public officials or private citizens, should determine when it must be restricted."[16]

Because the FOIA covers the entire executive branch, many of the most significant cases interpreting the FOIA have little or nothing to do with environmental information. They are important to any discussion of access to environmental information because the rules established under the case law also apply in cases involving environmental access. As passed in 1966, the original FOIA included weaknesses that detracted from its ideal operation.[17] There was initially little or no way, for instance, for a FOIA requester to determine whether an agency had fully complied with a request. In response, courts fashioned procedural devices, such as the requirement of a "Vaughn Index,"[18] established in *Vaughn v. Rosen.*[19] The "Vaughn Index" is a thorough index of each "FOIA request" and is compiled by each agency. It lists all of the documents that are withheld from the public and the justification for their exemption.[20] Similarly, the U.S. Supreme Court in *EPA v. Mink*[21] held that each agency must release to the public any segregable, nonexempt portions of a partially exempt record.[22]

In reaction to the abuses of the Watergate era,[23] and in an effort to expand the FOIA's disclosure requirements, Congress substantially amended the Act in 1974.[24] Those amendments considerably narrowed the scope of the FOIA's law enforcement and national security exemptions and expanded many of the agency procedural requirements, such as those regarding fees, time limits, segregability, and in camera inspection by the courts.[25] In 1976, Congress acted to further limit what could be withheld by agencies as exempt from disclosure under the FOIA, by limiting the circumstances under which an agency can rely on other statutes to withhold information.[26]

In 1986, after the FOIA had been in force for just over twenty years, Congress responded to a perceived need for reform of both the substantive and procedural requirements of the statute by enacting the Freedom of Information Reform Act of 1986.[27] The Reform Act of 1986 amended the FOIA "to provide broader exemption protection for law enforcement information, plus special law enforcement record exclusions, and also created a new fee and fee waiver structure."[28]

The most recent changes to the FOIA came about with passage of the Electronic Freedom of Information Act Amendments (1996 amendments).[29] The 1996 amendments addressed electronic records, such as electronic mail retained by agencies, as well as FOIA reading rooms and procedural time limits for agency processing.[30] Under the 1996 amendments, when responding to FOIA requests, each agency must search electronic databases for the requested records "except when such efforts would significantly interfere with the operation of the agency's automated information system."[31]

The FOIA Today

The FOIA, in general, requires federal agencies, including the military services, to provide the fullest possible disclosure of information to the public.[32] The FOIA provides a means for citizens to acquire all types of governmental information, unless a specific exemption applies.[33] While some types of information, particularly environmental information, may also have other disclosure requirements, the FOIA provides a means for accessing information in situations where no other means of access is provided.[34] It does so by establishing a presumption that all agency records and documents are accessible to the public.[35] It sets standards for determining which records must be disclosed by federal agencies and which records can be withheld.[36] The law provides both administrative and judicial remedies for individuals or groups who are denied access to records.[37] The FOIA applies to all agencies of the federal executive branch.[38] This includes each of the government departments and all subordinate agencies.[39] It does not apply to the U.S. Congress or to the federal judiciary.[40] It also does not apply to state or local government entities.[41]

The FOIA also requires each agency to establish "reading rooms" that must be accessible to the public.[42] Three categories of information must be included in an agency's reading room. Those broad categories include "final opinions . . . rendered in the adjudication of administrative cases, specific agency policy statements, and certain administrative staff manuals."[43] Reading room records must be indexed by the agencies to facilitate public access.[44] In addition to those materials, agencies must make available any records that were sought and obtained through the FOIA process that the agency determines will likely be requested again.[45] Under the 1996 amendments, each agency is required to make all records that are created after November 1, 1996, available electronically by December 31, 1999.[46] The rationale for reading rooms is that public access to such records serves to guard against development of "secret agency law," which is known to agency employees but not to the general public.[47] Agencies have also used their FOIA reading rooms to achieve "affirmative" disclosure of records that would otherwise likely be the subject of FOIA requests.[48]

The FOIA requires anyone who requests information to ask for existing agency records rather than general information.[49] An "agency record," according to the U.S. Supreme Court, is a document that is (1) either created or obtained by an agency and (2) under agency control at the time of the request.[50] Thus, an agency is only required to look for existing records in response to a FOIA request.[51] If no record exists, the agency is under no obligation to create one, collect information that it does not possess, perform research, or analyze data for a requester.[52] Any document containing information that is in the control of an agency, including electronic mail, is generally considered to be an agency record.[53] The form of the record maintained by the agency does not affect its availability.[54]

To request records from an agency, a requester must "reasonably describe such records" being sought.[55] In other words, the request must be specific enough to permit a government employee to locate the record in a reasonable period of time.[56] "The legislative history of the 1974 FOIA amendments indicates that a description of a requested record is sufficient if it enables a professional agency employee familiar with the subject area to locate the record with a 'reasonable amount of effort.'"[57] Agency officials are not expected to become "full time investigators" under the FOIA. Thus, a FOIA request will be held invalid if it requires an agency's FOIA staff either to have "clairvoyant capabilities" to infer the requester's desires or to spend "countless numbers of personnel hours seeking needles in bureaucratic haystacks."[58] Nevertheless, an agency "must be careful not to read [a] request so strictly that the requester is denied information the agency well knows exists in its files, albeit in a different form than that anticipated by the requester."[59] The fact that the records sought might be voluminous in nature does not absolve the agency of its duty to provide them.[60] The key factor, according to the U.S. Department of Justice (DOJ), "is the ability of an agency's staff to reasonably ascertain which records are being requested and locate them."[61] If the requester is not sure how to identify a specific record or records, he or she may phrase the request more broadly. For example, he or she may request "all records pertaining to" a specific, narrowly limited topic with sufficient detail to allow agency employees to determine what records may be the target of the search.[62]

Each agency has twenty working days[63] after the receipt of a FOIA request to determine whether or not to comply with the request, and then respond to the requester.[64] The initial response may simply indicate that the agency needs an additional ten working days to process the request because of "unusual circumstances," such as having to collect records at a remote location, to pore over voluminous amounts of records, or to consult with other agencies.[65] A requester may, however, seek expedited processing by claiming either (1) that failure to obtain records quickly will pose an imminent threat to the life or safety of an individual or (2) that, for journalist requesters, it can be shown that the request involves urgent matters about government activities that must be disseminated to the public as quickly as possible.[66]

Those requesting agency records under the FOIA may have to pay fees covering some or all of the costs of processing their requests.[67] Under the FOIA, each agency is required to promulgate FOIA regulations that specify "the schedule of fees applicable to the processing of requests under this section and [establish] procedures and guidelines for determining when such fees should be waived or reduced."[68] Those "fees shall be limited to reasonable standard charges for document search, duplication, and review, when records are requested for commercial use."[69] When a representative of the news media or an educational or noncommercial scientific institution for scholarly or scientific research makes the request, the "fees shall be limited to reasonable standard charges for document duplication," but search and review charges shall not apply.[70] When the requester fits into neither of the first two categories—commercial or news media/research—fees are "limited to reasonable standard charges for document search and duplication" but not for review.[71] Also, the agency has discretion to waive or reduce charges entirely if it determines that "disclosure of the information is in the public interest because it is likely to contribute significantly to public understanding of the operations or activities of the government and is not primarily in the commercial interest of the requester."[72]

Exemptions

There are nine statutory exemptions under which an agency may refuse to disclose agency records, either in whole or in part.[73] The exemptions address disclosure of information that would harm national defense or foreign policy, privacy of individuals, proprietary interests of business, functioning of the government, law enforcement investigations, and other important interests.[74] Any "reasonably segregable portion of a record," however, must be provided to the requester after "deletion of the portions which are exempt."[75]

Under appropriate circumstances, any of the exemptions might be used to withhold information pertaining directly or indirectly to the military's impacts on the environment or compliance with environmental laws.

Exemption 1 of the FOIA protects classified documents, defined as documents authorized to be kept secret because of their sensitive nature "in the interest of national defense or foreign policy."[76] The documents, however, must be properly classified in accordance with an executive order.[77] Under the executive order, information may not be classified unless its "disclosure . . . reasonably could be expected to result in damage to the national security."[78] After the tragedy of September 11, 2001, President George W. Bush expanded the categories of classified information to include information that should be withheld in the interest of homeland security.[79] Information categories that may not be considered as bases for information include diplomatic and foreign relations information; foreign government information; nuclear technology; intelligence activities; "military plans, weapons systems, or operations; . . . scientific, technological, or economic matters relating to the national security, which includes defense against transnational terrorism; . . . vulnerabilities or capabilities of systems, installations, infrastructures, projects, plans or protection services relating to the national security; [and] . . . weapons of mass destruction."[80]

Although the categories of permissible classified materials were broadened by the Bush administration's 2003 amendment, Executive Order 12,958 does not contain a "catch-all" provision for classification of other kinds of information, as its predecessor had.[81] In addition, Executive Order 12,958 eliminated the presumption that certain kinds of information, such as foreign government information, are classified.[82] As with two prior orders, the current executive order also prohibits classification to "conceal violations of law, inefficiency or administrative error, [to] prevent embarrassment to a person or agency," or to classify information for any other reasons not related to the national security.[83] If the agency's affidavits in support of classifying information are "reasonably specific" and there is no evidence of bad faith, the agency's determination will generally be upheld without an in camera review of the documents.[84] If this is not the case, however, courts have authority under the FOIA to review agency documents in camera to determine the propriety of withholding the documents.[85]

Exemption 2 addresses internal agency personnel rules and practices.[86] These rules govern internal agency conduct but not public behavior. This exemption encompasses two categories of information: "internal matters of a relatively trivial nature" and "more substantial internal matters, the disclosure of which would risk circumvention of a legal requirement."[87] The "trivial matters" category includes only "internal personnel rules and practices of an agency."[88] "Examples of these may be rules as to personnel's use of parking facilities or regulation of lunch hours, statements of policy as to sick leave, and the like."[89] The "more substantial matters" category applies to documents that are "predominantly internal" in nature, the disclosure of which "significantly risks circumvention of agency regulations or statutes."[90] Under this rationale, an agency's decision not to disclose a law enforcement agent's training manual has been upheld.[91] Under this rule, individual qualifications, or the lack thereof, of commanders or other officials responsible for environmental programs could potentially be withheld, although it is difficult to envision a motive for doing so.

Exemption 3 addresses documents that are exempted from disclosure under other federal statues.[92] These include only documents that are specifically required by another statute to be kept confidential, leaving "no discretion on the issue," or documents that meet specific criteria for withholding under another statute.[93] In the original FOIA, Exemption 3 was phrased so as to broadly exempt information "specifically exempted from disclosure by statute."[94] The U.S. Supreme Court, in *Federal Aviation Administration v. Robertson*,[95] interpreted this language to allow access to information under statutes that permitted the discretionary withholding of confidential information, enacted prior to the FOIA, to remain unaffected by the FOIA's broad requirements.[96] The Court thus upheld the agency's withholding documents in the "public interest," as permitted by the Federal Aviation Act.[97] Congress legislatively reversed the Court's decision by amending Exemption 3 in 1976 to prevent agencies from avoiding the FOIA's disclosure intent.[98] As amended, agencies may now invoke this exemption only if the claimed withholding statute either "(A) requires that the matters be withheld from the public in such a manner as to leave no discretion on the issue, or (B) establishes particular criteria for withholding or refers to particular types of matters to be withheld."[99] Without conforming to the specific exemption language in the claimed withholding statute, the records must be released.[100]

Exemption 4 pertains to business information specifically addressing "trade secrets and commercial or financial information obtained from a person and privileged or confidential."[101] It is "intended to protect the interests of both the government and submitters of information."[102] Exemption 4 could potentially apply to information submitted by defense contractors that would have implications for the environment. The exemption allows submitters of information, such as companies bidding for government contracts, to furnish sensitive commercial or financial information, and it provides assurance to the government that the information provided will be reliable. "The exemption covers two broad categories of information in federal agency records: (1) trade secrets; and (2) information which is: (a) commercial or financial, and

(b) obtained from a person, and (c) privileged or confidential."[103] The term "trade secret" has been narrowly defined by case law as "a secret, commercially valuable plan, formula, process, or device that is used for the making, preparing, compounding, or processing of trade commodities and that can be said to be the end product of either innovation or substantial effort."[104] The first two requirements of the second category of records are interpreted according to the "ordinary meanings" of the words.[105] Information is not considered to be "privileged or confidential" under the third requirement, however, unless disclosure of the information would either "(1) . . . impair the Government's ability to obtain necessary information in the future; or (2) . . . cause substantial harm to the competitive position of the person from whom the information was obtained."[106]

Exemption 5 addresses "inter-agency or intra-agency memorandums or letters which would not be available by law to a party . . . in litigation with the agency."[107] This type of information naturally includes attorney-client communications and information compiled in preparation for litigation.[108] The U.S. Supreme Court has interpreted coverage of Exemption 5 quite broadly, making it clear that the exemption includes "both statutory privileges and those commonly recognized by case law, and that it is not limited to those privileges explicitly mentioned in its legislative history."[109] According to the U.S. Justice Department, the most commonly asserted privilege under this exemption is the "deliberative process privilege"[110] That privilege protects predecisional information during the "decision making processes of government agencies."[111] The bases for this privilege are "(1) to encourage open, frank discussions on matters of policy between subordinates and superiors; (2) to protect against premature disclosure of proposed policies before they are finally adopted; and (3) to protect against public confusion that might result from disclosure of reasons and rationales that were not in fact ultimately the grounds for an agency's action."[112] To qualify for the deliberative process privilege, a communication must be both predecisional, that is, "antecedent to the adoption of an agency policy,"[113] and deliberative, that is, "a direct part of the deliberative process in that it makes recommendations or expresses opinions on legal or policy matters."[114] Deliberations of Department of Defense (DOD) agencies leading up to decisions on actions affecting the environment would likely qualify for this exemption, but the resulting decision would not.

Exemption 6 pertains to private matters, including "personnel and medical files and similar files the disclosure of which would constitute a clearly unwarranted invasion of personal privacy."[115] This exemption could be used to protect medical information from release of personnel who suffer from exposures to contamination on military installations. While "personal and medical files" are easily identified, courts initially struggled with the meaning of the term "similar files."[116] Prior to 1982, judicial interpretations of this term varied widely, but the U.S. Supreme Court settled the issue in its decision in *United States Department of State v. Washington Post Co.*[117] In this case, the Court held that Congress intended the term to be interpreted broadly.[118] The Court stressed that all information that "applies to a particular individual" meets the requirement for Exemption 6 protection.[119] The exemption can apply equally to the "author" and to the "subject" of a file.[120] The documents sought must still "constitute a clearly unwarranted invasion of personal privacy."[121] To determine whether an invasion of privacy is "unwarranted" requires a balancing "of the public's right to disclosure against the individual's right to privacy."[122] The Supreme Court in *United States Department of Justice v. Reporters Committee for Freedom of the Press*[123] established five principles to govern the process by which determinations are made under both Exemption 6 and Exemption 7(C).[124] First, substantial privacy interests can exist in personal information even if it has been available to the general public at some previous time.[125] Second, the identity of a FOIA requester[126] cannot be considered in determining what is appropriate for release under the FOIA (unless, of course, an individual is requesting personal information on him- or herself).[127] Third, in determining whether release of a document is in the public interest, the agency's decision "must turn on the nature of the requested document and its relationship" to the public interest.[128] Fourth, the scope of the public interest to be considered is limited to "the kind of public interest for which Congress enacted the FOIA," which is to shed "light on an agency's performance of its statutory duties."[129] Fifth, an agency may determine, "as a categorical matter," that certain types of information can always be protected under one of the privacy exemptions "without regard to individual circumstances."[130]

Next, FOIA Exemption 7 pertains to law enforcement investigations.[131] It permits withholding records compiled for law enforcement purposes but is limited to circumstances in which production of a document would potentially interfere with a law enforcement investigation, would prejudice an individual's ability to receive a fair trial, would constitute an "unwarranted invasion of personal privacy," would reveal the identity of a confidential source, would reveal techniques or procedures of investigations or prosecutions, or would "endanger the life or physical safety [of] any individual."[132] Any investigation into environmental crimes would qualify for this exemption to the FOIA.

In addition to the law enforcement exemption, when a FOIA request involves a criminal investigation for which the subject of the investigation is not aware and disclosure of the existence of records could interfere with enforcement proceedings, an agency may "treat the records as not subject to the requirements of this section."[133] In other words, the agency need neither admit nor deny the existence of the records.

Exemptions 8 and 9 are perhaps the least likely to apply to a FOIA request to any DOD agency for documents pertinent to the environment. Exemption 8 pertains to sensitive information maintained regarding financial institutions.[134] It permits the withholding of information that is "contained in or related to examination, operating or condition reports prepared by, on behalf of, or for the use of an agency responsible for the regulation or supervision of financial institutions."[135] Courts have identified two major purposes for Exemption 8. They are, first, "to protect the security of financial institutions by withholding from the public reports that contain frank evaluations of a bank's stability" and, second, "to promote cooperation and communication between employees and examiners."[136] Exemption 9 addresses "geological and geophysical information and data, including maps, concerning wells."[137] The purpose and meaning of Exemption 9 is obvious enough that, according to the U.S. Department of Justice, this is a rarely invoked or interpreted exemption, with very few reported cases.[138]

If the agency denies disclosure under one of the exemptions, it must "notify the person making such a request of such determination and the reasons therefore, and of the right of such person to appeal to the head of the agency any adverse determination."[139] The agency would then have twenty days to process any appeal.[140] Each year, every federal agency is required to provide a report to the U.S. Attorney General, which includes, among other things, "the number of determinations made by the agency not to comply with requests for records made to such agency . . . and the reasons for each such determination."[141] The attorney general must then make those reports available to the public by electronic means and notify Congress of their availability.[142]

If a record qualifies for one of the nine exemptions, however, the agency may not necessarily be required or allowed to withhold it.[143] During the Clinton administration, agencies were encouraged to provide information even if it could be withheld under one of the FOIA exemptions. Under a memorandum issued in 1993 to the heads of all executive agencies, Attorney General Janet Reno issued policy guidelines for processing FOIA requests.[144] In her message, she declared that the U.S. Department of Justice would "no longer defend an agency's withholding of information merely because there is 'substantial legal basis' for doing so. Rather, in determining whether or not to defend a nondisclosure decision, we will apply a presumption of disclosure."[145] She explained that, while the FOIA itself contemplates, through its exemptions, circumstances under which information should not be disclosed to the public because of harm to national and private interests, "I firmly believe that these exemptions are best applied with specific reference to such harm, and only after consideration of the reasonably expected consequences of disclosure in each particular case."[146] She adopted the policy that the Justice Department would only defend an assertion of a FOIA exemption by agencies "in those cases where the agency reasonably foresees that disclosure would be harmful to an interest protected by that exemption. Where an item of information might technically or arguably fall within an exemption, it ought not to be withheld from a FOIA requester unless it need be."[147] She further urged agency FOIA officers to make "discretionary disclosures" whenever possible, rather than withhold.[148] President Clinton echoed Attorney General Reno's sentiments: "The use of the Act by ordinary citizens is not complicated, nor should it be. The existence of unnecessary bureaucratic hurdles has no place in its implementation."[149] President Clinton also emphasized an agency's responsibility "to distribute information on its own initiative, and to enhance public access through the use of electronic information systems. Taking these steps will ensure compliance with both the letter and spirit of the Act."[150] This was a positive step in ensuring that agencies will not simply hide behind the FOIA exemptions to avoid releasing information.

But on October 12, 2001, Attorney General John Ashcroft overturned the Reno memorandum and issued his own.[151] Although reiterating the Department of Justice's commitment to "full compliance with the Freedom of Information Act," the Ashcroft memorandum stated that the DOJ would defend any agency's withholding of documents under FOIA exemptions as long as there was a "sound legal basis" for doing so.[152] The Ashcroft memorandum changed the emphasis on FOIA decisions to encourage agencies to withhold documents covered by exemptions and to release documents "only after full and deliberate consideration of the institutional, commercial, and personal privacy interests that could be implicated by disclosure of the information."[153] Under the Ashcroft guidance, agencies no longer had to determine whether disclosure would be harmful to an interest protected by the exemption. The presumption shifted from a presumption for disclosure to a presumption for withholding documents. This appeared to be a major shift in policy away from open government principles. However, in 2003 the General Accounting Office (GAO—now known as the Government Accountability Office) issued a report that agency FOIA officers did not notice changes in their agencies' responses to FOIA requests in comparison to previous years.[154] According to the report, about a third of the FOIA officers reported a decreased likelihood of their agency making discretionary disclosures, with about 75 percent of them citing the Ashcroft memorandum as the reason.[155] Some 62 percent of FOIA officers reported no change as a result of the Ashcroft memorandum.[156] The GAO report did not disclose whether the defense and national security agencies were among the agencies reporting a reduced likelihood of discretionary disclosure.

Nevertheless, the Ashcroft memorandum reflects a significantly different emphasis—shifting markedly away from government openness toward the national defense—than its predecessor. While such a shift is understandable in the wake of the terrorist threat to the United States, it is important to ensure that our citizens' access to environmental information is not unnecessarily eclipsed.

The Power of the FOIA

The Freedom of Information Act can give the power of government back to the people. Only an informed electorate can hold its government accountable. By contrast, unnecessary secrecy in government, particularly with regard to environmental issues that can affect many people, can lead to arrogance in governance and defective decision making. It can be a great hindrance to public awareness and as a result become a corrosive influence in the decline of public confidence in government. It makes it more difficult for the public to hold the defense agencies accountable for their actions. Yet, a balance must be struck between information access and national security. When the government keeps information secret, it fuels the fear that environmental problems are not handled in a fair and equitable manner. "The military's unrestrained urge to 'go dark,' as its covert operatives might say, will inevitably undermine public trust in its credibility and integrity, especially because the military's environmental track record is mixed, its good faith suspect, and the stakes for public health and the environment very high," wrote several commentators critical of the post–September 11, 2001, information policy.[157] This distrust can lead to disregard for the law if members of the public draw conclusions, based on incomplete information, that the government does not enforce and observe the law evenhandedly, or at all.

There is a perception in the United States that the military agencies are unnecessarily favored in environmental law. Public awareness is one of the avenues the military services can use to erase this perception. By making information on its considerable environmental efforts available to the public, the military services can show that they are good environmental neighbors and stewards. Yet, the Ashcroft memorandum tends to reverse the sound policy of releasing information, including environmental information, unless it is absolutely necessary to withhold it. But the agencies still have the discretion to release information if they deem it appropriate to do so. In spite of the Ashcroft memorandum, it may be in the long-term interest of the military services—and the nation—for them to disclose information, particularly environmental information, as freely as the national security allows.

Notes

1. Lotte E. Feinberg, *The Day LBJ Signed FOIA*, QUILL 13–15 (Oct. 1996).
2. *Id.*
3. See *id.*
4. Freedom of Information Act, Pub. L. No. 89-487, 80 Stat. 250 (1966).
5. Feinberg, *The Day LBJ Signed FOIA*, supra note 1, at 15.
6. *Id.*
7. *Id.*
8. H.R. 2767, 85th Cong. (1958); see also Laura Schenck, *Freedom of Information Statutes: The Unfulfilled Legacy*, 48 FED. COMM. L.J. 371, 374 (1995).
9. H.R. 2767, 85th Cong. (1958); see also Schenck, *Freedom of Information*, supra note 8, at 374.
10. Freedom of Information Act, § 3.
11. *Id.* § 3(e).
12. *Id.* § 3.
13. Statement by the President upon Signing the "Freedom of Information Act," 316 Pub. Papers, supra note 596, at 699 (July 4, 1966).
14. See *id.*
15. *Id.*
16. *Id.*
17. U.S. DEPARTMENT OF JUSTICE, FREEDOM OF INFORMATION ACT GUIDE (May 2004), www.usdoj.gov/04foia/foi-act.htm.
18. *Id.*
19. Vaughn v. Rosen, 484 F.2d 820, 827 (D.C. Cir. 1973).
20. U.S. DEPARTMENT OF JUSTICE, FREEDOM OF INFORMATION ACT GUIDE, supra note 17.
21. EPA v. Mink, 410 U.S. 73, 91 (1973).
22. U.S. DEPARTMENT OF JUSTICE, FREEDOM OF INFORMATION ACT GUIDE, supra note 17. This requirement was later adopted into the FOIA and is now codified at 5 U.S.C. § 552(b). "Any reasonably segregable portion of a record shall be provided to any person requesting such record after deletion of the portions which are exempt under this subsection."
23. U.S. DEPARTMENT OF JUSTICE, FREEDOM OF INFORMATION ACT GUIDE, supra note 17.
24. *Id.*
25. *Id.*; Freedom of Information Act (Amendments), 1561, 1561–64.
26. Government in the Sunshine Act, Pub. L. No. 94-409, 90 Stat. 1247 (1976).
27. 5 U.S.C. § 552.
28. U.S. DEPARTMENT OF JUSTICE, FREEDOM OF INFORMATION ACT GUIDE, supra note 17.
29. Electronic Freedom of Information Act Amendments of 1996, Pub. L. No. 104-231, 110 Stat. 3048 (1986).
30. See *id.*
31. *Id.* § 5(4)(c).
32. See, generally, Freedom of Information Act, § 3.
33. *Id.*

34. *Id.*
35. *Id.* § 3(a)–(d).
36. *Id.* § 3(e)–(f).
37. *Id.* § 3(c).
38. 5 U.S.C. § 552. When the then-new U.S. Environmental Protection Agency first unveiled its regulations for complying with the FOIA, those regulations were heralded as a model for other government agencies. Frederick P. McBrier, *The EPA's Proposed Rule for Freedom of Information Act Disclosures: A Model for Orderly Agency Determinations*, UTAH L. REV. 943, 961 (1975).
39. 5 U.S.C. § 551(1).
40. *Id.* § 551(1)(A)–(B).
41. 5 U.S.C. § 551(1)(C).
42. 5 U.S.C. § 552(a)(2). "Subsection (a)(2) of the FOIA provides for what is commonly referred to as 'reading room' access" (U.S. DEPARTMENT OF JUSTICE, FREEDOM OF INFORMATION ACT GUIDE, supra note 17).
43. U.S. DEPARTMENT OF JUSTICE, FREEDOM OF INFORMATION ACT GUIDE, supra note 17.
44. 5 U.S.C. § 552(a)(2)(c).
45. *Id.* § 552(a)(2).
46. *Id.*
47. *Id.* § 552(a)(1)–(a)(2).
48. *Id.*
49. Freedom of Information Act, § 3(c).
50. United States Department of Justice v. Tax Analysts, 492 U.S. 136, 144–45 (1989).
51. See *id.* at 145–46.
52. See *id.*
53. *Id.* at 145.
54. *Id.*
55. 5 U.S.C. § 552(a)(3)(A).
56. U.S. DEPARTMENT OF JUSTICE, FREEDOM OF INFORMATION ACT GUIDE, supra note 17.
57. *Id.*
58. *Id.*
59. Hemenway v. Hughes, 601 F. Supp. 1002, 1005 (D.D.C. 1985).
60. U.S. DEPARTMENT OF JUSTICE, FREEDOM OF INFORMATION ACT GUIDE, supra note 17.
61. *Id.*
62. *Id.*
63. *Id.* at 40–41.
64. 5 U.S.C. § 552(a)(6)(A).
65. *Id.* § 552(a)(6)(B).
66. 5 U.S.C. § 552(a)(6)(E)(v)(I).
67. *Id.* § 552(a)(4)(I).
68. *Id.*
69. *Id.* § 552(a)(4)(A)(ii)(I).
70. *Id.* § 552(a)(4)(A)(ii)(II).
71. *Id.* § 552(a)(4)(A)(ii)(III).
72. *Id.* § 552(a)(4)(A)(iii).

73. *Id.* § 552(b)(1)–(9).
74. See, generally, *id.* § 552(b).
75. *Id.*
76. *Id.* § 552(b)(1)(A).
77. *Id.* § 552(b)(1)(B). The order currently in effect is Exec. Order 12,958, 3 C.F.R. 335 (1995). This executive order replaced Exec. Order 12,356, 3 C.F.R. 166 (1983), and has itself been amended a number of times, including a major amendment by Exec. Order 13,292 on Mar. 28, 2003 (68 Fed. Reg. 15315).
78. Exec. Order No. 12,958, as amended by Exec. Order No. 13,292, § 1.1(4) (2003).
79. *Id.*
80. *Id.* § 1.4.
81. SEE U.S. DEPARTMENT OF JUSTICE, FREEDOM OF INFORMATION ACT GUIDE, supra note 17.
82. *Id.*
83. Exec. Order No. 12,958, as amended by Exec. Order No. 13,292, § 1.7(a) (2003).
84. SEE U.S. DEPARTMENT OF JUSTICE, FREEDOM OF INFORMATION ACT GUIDE, supra note 17.
85. 5 U.S.C. § 552(a)(4)(B).
86. *Id.* § 552 (b)(2).
87. U.S. DEPARTMENT OF JUSTICE, FREEDOM OF INFORMATION ACT GUIDE, supra note 17.
88. *Id.*
89. S. Rep. No. 89-813, at 8 (1965).
90. Crooker v. Bureau of Alcohol, Tobacco and Firearms, 670 F. 2d 1051, 1073–74 (D.C. Cir. 1981).
91. *Id.* at 1074.
92. U.S. DEPARTMENT OF JUSTICE, FREEDOM OF INFORMATION ACT GUIDE, supra note 17.
93. 5 U.S.C. § 552(b)(3).
94. Freedom of Information Act.
95. Federal Aviation Administration v. Robertson, 422 U.S. 255 (1975).
96. See *id.* at 266.
97. *Id.*
98. Government in the Sunshine Act; see also U.S. DEPARTMENT OF JUSTICE, FREEDOM OF INFORMATION ACT GUIDE, supra note 17.
99. 5 U.S.C. § 552(b)(3).
100. U.S. DEPARTMENT OF JUSTICE, FREEDOM OF INFORMATION ACT GUIDE, supra note 17.
101. 5 U.S.C. § 552(b)(4).
102. U.S. DEPARTMENT OF JUSTICE, FREEDOM OF INFORMATION ACT GUIDE, supra note 17.
103. *Id.* (emphasis added).
104. Public Citizen Health Research Group v. FDA, 704 F.2d 1280, 1288 (D.C. Cir. 1983).
105. U.S. DEPARTMENT OF JUSTICE, FREEDOM OF INFORMATION ACT GUIDE, supra note 17.

106. National Parks and Conservation Association v. Morton, 498 F.2d 765, 770 (D.C. Cir. 1974).

107. 5 U.S.C. § 552(b)(5).

108. U.S. DEPARTMENT OF JUSTICE, FREEDOM OF INFORMATION ACT GUIDE, supra note 17.

109. *Id.*

110. *Id.*

111. National Labor Relations Board v. Sears, Roebuck & Co., 421 U.S. 132, 150 (1975).

112. U.S. DEPARTMENT OF JUSTICE, FREEDOM OF INFORMATION ACT GUIDE, supra note 17.

113. Jordan v. United States Department of Justice, 591 F.2d 753, 772–74 (D.C. Cir. 1978).

114. Vaughn v. Rosen, 523 F.2d 1136, 1143–44 (D.C. Cir. 1975).

115. 5 U.S.C § 552(b)(6).

116. See United States Department of State v. Washington Post Co., 456 U.S. 595 (1982).

117. *Id.*

118. See *id.* at 602.

119. See *id.*

120. See New York Times Co. v. NASA, 920 F.2d 1002, 1007–8 (D.C. Cir. 1990).

121. U.S. DEPARTMENT OF JUSTICE, FREEDOM OF INFORMATION ACT GUIDE, supra note 17.

122. *Id.* at 259.

123. United States Department of Justice v. Reporters Committee for Freedom of Press, 489 U.S. 749 (1989).

124. See *id.*

125. See *id.* at 762–64.

126. *Id.* at 771.

127. *Id.*

128. *Id.* at 772.

129. *Id.* at 773–74.

130. *Id.* at 780.

131. 5 U.S.C. § 552(b)(7).

132. *Id.*

133. *Id.* § 552(c)(1).

134. *Id.* § 552(b)(8).

135. *Id.*

136. Atkinson v. FDIC, 1 G.D.S. P 80,034, P 80,102 (D.D.C. 1980).

137. 5 U.S.C. § 552(b)(9).

138. U.S. DEPARTMENT OF JUSTICE, FREEDOM OF INFORMATION ACT GUIDE, supra note 17.

139. 5 U.S.C. § 552(a)(6)(A)(i).

140. *Id.*

141. *Id.* § 552(e)(1)(A).

142. *Id.* § 552(e)(3).

143. See *id.* § 552(d).

144. Attorney General Janet Reno, Memorandum on the Freedom of Information Act, to Heads of Departments and Agencies (Oct. 4, 1993).

145. *Id.* at 1.

146. *Id.*

147. *Id.*

148. *Id.*

149. William J. Clinton, Memorandum on the Freedom of Information Act, 2 Pub. Papers 1685 (Oct. 4, 1993).

150. *Id.*

151. Attorney General John Ashcroft, Memorandum on the Freedom of Information Act, to Heads of Departments and Agencies (Oct. 12, 2001).

152. *Id.*

153. *Id.*

154. U.S. GENERAL ACCOUNTING OFFICE, REPORT TO THE RANKING MINORITY MEMBER, COMMITTEE ON THE JUDICIARY, U.S. SENATE, FREEDOM OF INFORMATION ACT: AGENCY VIEWS ON CHANGES RESULTING FROM NEW ADMINISTRATION POLICY (Sept. 2003).

155. *Id.* at 2.

156. *Id.* at 3.

157. Christopher Gozdor, Shana Campbell Jones, Kristen Klick, and Matthew Steinhilber, *Where the Streets Have No Name: The Collision of Environmental Law and Information Policy in the Age of Terrorism*, 33 ELR 10978 (2003).

III

WARTIME OPERATIONS

10

The Nature of War

War itself, fought by legitimate means, can be devastating to the environment. Fought by illegitimate means, it can be even more deadly. Men have for centuries used the environment as a weapon in warfare, including the Union Army's "scorched earth" policy during the U.S. Civil War and the United States' widespread use of herbicides to deny concealment during the Vietnam War.[1] During Operation Desert Storm in 1991, thousands of combat sorties were flown and hundreds of cruise missiles were launched against Iraqi troops within the first days of the conflict. In response to the onslaught by the United States and its coalition allies, Iraqi leader Saddam Hussein responded by unleashing a massive oil spill into the Persian Gulf and setting devastating oil well fires. It was feared at the time that the long-range environmental damages of that war could never be ameliorated.[2] Hussein's ability to mete such devastation against the environment without apparent retribution caused many international observers to wonder whether international law was sufficient to address such a massive environmental attack. It sparked a debate that continues to this day that involves a philosophical examination not only of the intentional infliction of harm on the environment, such as Hussein's, but also the routine environmental damage that results from using high-tech, highly destructive weapons for the purposes they were intended.[3]

The International Emergence of Environmental Values

The recognition of environmental values in international law has been a relatively recent development. Although some formal peacetime international agreements regarding the environment—such as the 1954 International Convention for the Prevention of Pollution of the Sea by Oil—date back a half century, to Sonja Ann Jozef Boelaert-Suominen and the United Nations' Conference on the Human Environment, convened in Stockholm in 1972, which marked the emergence of environmental protection principles in international law.[4] Dr. Boelaert-Suominen, legal advisor in the Office of the Prosecutor for the International Criminal Tribunal for the former Yugoslavia, pointed to the Stockholm Declaration of Principles for the Preservation and Enhancement of the Human Environment as a milestone in modern international environmental law. The Stockholm Declaration, which consisted of a preamble and twenty-six principles, was adopted in conjunction with the 109 recommendations of the Action Plan for the Human Environment. Of paramount importance among the Stockholm Declaration's principles is Principle 21, which enunciates that nations have "the sovereign right to exploit their own resources pursuant to their own environmental policies, and the responsibility to ensure that the activities within their jurisdiction or control do not cause damage to the environment of other States or of areas beyond the limits of national jurisdiction."[5]

Many subsequent international agreements have established the tradition that during peacetime nations have a responsibility to act in a manner that is environmentally responsible to other nations. "The duty of international cooperation can be said to underlie all international (environmental) law," Dr. Boelaert-Suominen wrote. "Pursuant to this requirement, States need to cooperate in mitigating environmental risks and emergencies."[6] It is within the framework of international law that we now view environmental damage during war. But we must look through a separate lens—one that doesn't necessarily follow peacetime international law principles. Yet, the development of peacetime international environmental law is instructive in that it illuminates a greater emphasis on and sensitivity to environmental protection within the international community. Further, as Dr. Boelaert-Suominen has pointed out, "There is a strong tendency in modern international State practice, case law, and legal theory towards maintaining the validity of treaties insofar as compatible with national policy and with obligations stemming from Security Council decisions."[7] With greater value among all nations being placed on environmental protection, and a more robust peacetime international environmental law, one can anticipate that a belligerent nation's conduct toward the environment during warfare might be viewed with greater scrutiny. The extreme conduct of the Iraqi forces during the 1991 Gulf War drove the notion of environmental protection in warfare to the forefront of world consciousness.

The 1991 Persian Gulf War's Extreme Environmental Damage

On August 2, 1990, about 80,000 Iraqi troops invaded the small neighboring country of Kuwait.[8] After a massive deployment of troops, the United States and its 28 coalition allies launched a counterattack against the Iraqi forces on January 17, 1991—or January 16 in the United States. What ensued was an unprecedented air bombardment against Iraq that lasted for 40 days. Because of the devastation of the air war, the four-day ground assault launched on February 24, 1991, met little resistance from Iraqi forces.[9] The war not only astounded the world by its swiftness and decisiveness but also raised doubts about the sufficiency of international law to prevent environmental crimes in combat.

The first war with Iraq was fought by opposing forces that were vastly different in both capabilities and tactics. Coalition forces benefited from technological warfare that included cruise missiles, stealth bombers, and smart bombs. After the first hours of the conflict, coalition forces had achieved air superiority and largely devastated Iraq's internal command and control capabilities. Within 14 hours, more than 1,000 combat sorties were flown and more than 100 cruise missiles were launched against Iraqi targets.[10] The technological advantages of the coalition forces contributed to the astonishingly low casualties—about 350—suffered by the allied forces.[11] While estimates of Iraqi casualties were not officially made by the U.S. Department of Defense, unofficial estimates placed Iraqi war deaths at more than 100,000.[12]

While coalition forces attacked with technology that seemed to breach the next century, the response of overmatched Iraqi leader Saddam Hussein provided a stark contrast. "Saddam reacted in what seemed a different era of warfare," wrote Greenpeace military analysts, "with his own scorched earth destruction—unleashing one of the world's worst oil spills, and setting almost 600 oil wells ablaze."[13] Air bombardments in subsequent U.S. military efforts in Kosovo and the 2003 war in Iraq resulted in predictable environmental harm, but Hussein's acts during Desert Storm still stand alone because of their flagrant and intentional infliction of environmental damage. Although the total long-term impact of Iraqi environmental treachery was not readily known, the immediate impact was obvious and dramatic. The cumulative impact of the oil spills severely damaged Saudi Arabian shrimp beds and inflicted heavy damage on sea birds, turtles, and coral reefs.[14] "Whilst the exact size of the oil slick is debated, it is generally regarded as the largest ever recorded in human history," wrote Dr. Boelaert-Suominen. "It ruined fishing grounds for many countries in the region, and made beaches unsuitable for the tourist industry. The oil slick caused serious pollution of the Kuwaiti and Saudi Arabian coasts, and seriously threatened the latter's desalinization plants and offshore oil operations."[15] In addition, oil fires blackened the sky over Kuwait, spewing sulfurous gases and toxic particles into the air for about a year.[16]

Because of the impact the 1991 Persian Gulf War had on the natural environment, international and environmental legal scholars once again began examining the effectiveness of international laws of war at deterring environmental devastation during wartime. Greenpeace International, for instance, suggested that the Iraqi leadership could have been charged with environmental war crimes because of the intentional oil spills into the Persian Gulf and the sabotage to the Kuwaiti oil wells.[17] Greenpeace, however, also turned its microscope back toward the damage done to Iraq by coalition forces in the first invasion of Iraq by the United States and its allies and concluded that coalition forces made every attempt to comply with the laws of war such as they were.[18] "A conventional view of allied conduct," a Greenpeace study stated, "must conclude that allied military forces were within the letter of most of the laws of war as they currently stand."[19] Yet, its surprising conclusion was to suggest that the laws of war were, therefore, insufficient because of the devastation and discomfort suffered by Iraq's population.[20] "The traditional and conventional laws of war," the study concluded, "which center on the assumption of humanitarian conduct without restraining war itself, are an incomplete guide to moral behavior in the modern world."[21] In other words, because the coalition's efforts were so successful and so devastating, this is evidence that the laws of war should curb the very devastation of war itself.

Subsequent conflicts, such as the North Atlantic Treaty Organization (NATO) 1999 bombing campaign to suppress Serbian oppression of ethnic Albanians in Kosovo and the United States' Invasion of Iraq in 2003, also had significant environmental impacts. Absent the environmental crimes that distinguished the 1991 Persian Gulf War, these conflicts highlighted the severity of environmental damages inherent in modern warfare, which one commentator attributed to two factors. "First, the overall burden placed on the environment by human civilization is immeasurably greater than it was in the times of the Romans or of Moses," wrote Professor Aaron Schwabach. "Second, the capacity of humanity's weapons and implements of war to injure the environment is also immeasurably greater; it is possible for unrestrained use of chemical, nuclear, and biological weapons to render countries, continents, and even the entire planet uninhabitable."[22]

The infliction of environmental harm by legitimate means of warfare is a continuing concern among international law scholars. Concerns over the environmental consequences of military action persisted long after the 2003 Iraq War and included concerns over hangover effects from the 1991 conflict. A 2005 United Nations report, for instance, noted significant contamination due to bombing by coalition forces. "Military targeting of industrial sites typically produces severe, localized chemical contamination, while the associated secondary explosions, chemical releases and fires can result in high levels of air pollution in the short term," stated the report. "Given the recent history of Iraq, conflict-related chemical contamination is potentially a significant issue."[23] There were also unintended environmental consequences of the 2003 invasion. In the aftermath of the invasion, looters raided the Iraq Ministry of Agriculture's central pesticide storage facility at Al Suwaira, smashing pesticide containers, spreading contamination throughout the facility, and creating an unknown public health risk as hazardous pesticides were distributed uncontrolled into the population.[24] These consequences to industrial facilities occurred despite the allied forces' general avoidance of targeting nondefense industrial facilities during the 2003 invasion.[25]

In addition, new concerns over the impact of depleted uranium from armor-piercing rounds fired by the U.S. military during the conflicts against Kosovo and Iraq have accompanied the traditional concerns over environmental damages that are inherent in the violent nature of warfare.[26] Depleted uranium is a by-product of the uranium fuel enrichment process, which contains lower concentrations of radioisotopes than was contained in the natural uranium ore.[27] Depleted uranium is useful in some military munitions and armor because of its high density and strength.[28] Although radioactive levels of depleted uranium materials are considered too low to be a general environmental threat, special handling is required to avoid contamination.[29] And some Iraqi doctors reportedly believe that depleted uranium left behind by the U.S. military incident to its attacks on Iraqi troops in 1991 have contributed to a spike in cancer rates and birth defects among Iraqi civilians—perhaps another unforeseen consequence of military conflict.[30] The depleted uranium issue, wrote one commentator, "is likely to remain a volatile issue in the years to come.... Plainly and simply, depleted uranium is a toxic waste that has the potential to cause adverse health and environmental effects; therefore its use in large quantities near populated areas requires remedial action."[31]

But environmental impacts were collateral damage and not the primary objective in the conflict in Yugoslavia, in the invasion of Afghanistan, and in 2003's Operation Iraqi Freedom. The actions of the Iraqi forces during Operation Desert Storm are still in a class by themselves. "The situation in Yugoslavia differs from that in the two major wartime environmental incidents of recent times—the defoliation of Vietnam's forests and the incineration of Kuwait's oil," wrote Professor Schwabach. "In each of the latter two incidents, the environment itself was a target; the state committing the environmental harm deliberately set out to do so. In Yugoslavia, as is most commonly the case, the environmental damage was incidental to the achievement of some other objective."[32]

Notes

1. See, generally, Laurent R. Hourcle, *Environmental Law of War*, 25 VT. L. REV. 653 (2001).
2. WILLIAM M. ARKIN, DAMIAN DURRANT, AND MARIANNE CHERNI, ON IMPACT: MODERN WARFARE AND THE ENVIRONMENT—A CASE STUDY OF THE GULF WAR 25 (1991) (prepared by Greenpeace for a roundtable conference organized by Greenpeace International; Centre for Defence Studies, Kings College; and the London School of Economics).
3. For a comprehensive examination of environmental issues in warfare, see, e.g., CARL BRUCH AND JAY AUSTIN, EDS., THE ENVIRONMENTAL CONSEQUENCES OF WAR: LEGAL, ECONOMIC AND SCIENTIFIC PERSPECTIVES (2000).
4. SONJA ANN JOZEF BOELAERT-SUOMINEN, INTERNATIONAL ENVIRONMENTAL LAW AND NAVAL WAR 4 (2000) (Newport Paper Number Fifteen, Center for Naval Warfare Studies, Naval War College).
5. *Id.* at 22 (quoting UN Doc. A/CONF 48/14 and Corr. 1 [1972], www.unep.org/Documents.multilingual/Default.asp?DocumentID=97&ArticleID=1503 [accessed February 26, 2006]).
6. *Id.* at 25–26.
7. *Id.* at 136.
8. ARKIN, DURRANT, AND CHERNI, ON IMPACT, supra note 2, at 25.
9. *Id.* at 34–37.
10. *Id.* at 29.
11. *Id.* at 6.
12. *Id.*
13. *Id.* at 8.
14. Thomas P. Lippman, *Gulf War Leaves Environment Severely Wounded*, WASHINGTON POST, Mar. 2, 1991, at A1, col. 1.
15. BOELAERT-SUOMINEN, INTERNATIONAL ENVIRONMENTAL LAW, supra note 4, at 97.
16. Lippman, *Gulf War*, supra note 14, at A1.
17. ARKIN, DURRANT, AND CHERNI, ON IMPACT, supra note 2, at 21.
18. *Id.*
19. *Id.* at 146.
20. *Id.* at 22.
21. *Id.* at 146.

22. Aaron Schwabach, *Environmental Damage Resulting from the NATO Military Action against Yugoslavia*, 25 COLUM. J. ENVTL. L. 117, 121 (2000).

23. UNITED NATIONS ENVIRONMENT PROGRAMME, ASSESSMENT OF ENVIRONMENTAL "HOT SPOTS" IN IRAQ 34 (2005).

24. *Id.* at 74–76.

25. *Id.* at 35.

26. United Nations Environment Programme, Press Release, Apr. 24, 2003, www.unep.org/Documents.Multilingual/Default.asp?DocumentID=309&ArticleID=3965.

27. DEPARTMENT OF THE ARMY, REG. 700-48, MANAGEMENT OF EQUIPMENT CONTAMINATED WITH DEPLETED URANIUM OR RADIOACTIVE COMMODITIES 12 (Sept. 2002).

28. DEPARTMENT OF THE ARMY, TECHNICAL BULLETIN 9-1300-278, GUIDELINES FOR SAFE RESPONSE TO HANDLING, STORAGE, AND TRANSPORTATION ACCIDENTS INVOLVING ARMY TANK MUNITIONS OR ARMY WHICH CONTAIN DEPLETED URANIUM 1-1 (July 1996).

29. *Id.*

30. Larry Johnson, *Iraqi Cancers, Birth Defects Blamed on U.S. Depleted Uranium*, SEATTLE POST-INTELLIGENCER, Nov. 12, 2002.

31. Dan Fahey, *The Final Word on Depleted Uranium*, 25 FLETCHER F. WORLD AFF. 189, 189–190 (2001).

32. Schwabach, *Environmental Damage*, supra note 22, at 118.

11

The Laws of Armed Conflict and the Environment

THE ACTIONS OF THE IRAQIS during the 1991 Persian Gulf War were both shocking and unprecedented. Because of the intensity of the damages to the environment, and because no one was held responsible for the damages in the aftermath of the conflict, there has been concern that perhaps the international laws of war are insufficient to address such environmental damages. To punish the kind of environmental terrorism practiced by Iraqi forces during the 1991 Persian Gulf War, however, it is not necessary to enter into any new international agreements. Between customary international law and the Hague and Geneva conventions, the legal mechanisms have been in place that would enable any nation to charge Saddam Hussein and the senior Iraqi leadership at the time with environmental war crimes. U.S. Army Major Eric Talbot Jenson described efforts to use the environment as a weapon as "active environmental warfare."[1] To further expand international agreements to include prohibitions against environmental damage, as proposed by Greenpeace, is not necessary for the purpose of charging combatants with war crimes for intentional environmental damage.

In addition, amendments to or extensions of international law, if not properly drafted, might hinder an advanced nation's ability to conduct wartime operations with a minimum of casualties. During the United States' involvement in the 1991 Persian Gulf War, coalition forces were able to take advantage of superior technology and suffered only a few casualties when compared to enemy forces. The coalition's offensive was devastating on the enemy, but it was also efficient. It is impossible to determine whether other tactics, perhaps less damaging on the environment, would have been as effective in minimizing friendly casualties. New international agreements or amendments might have worked in the enemy's favor and caused more allied casualties if certain weapons or tactics were rendered illegal by the international agreements.

Customary International Laws of War

The foundations for international law, specifically the laws of war, can be found in customary international law. These are unwritten principles that generally have been followed by the world's military forces and accepted by all nations. While the formal agreement process did not begin until the second half of the nineteenth century, the specific codified rules did not displace customary law.[2] The modern agreements, in fact, have expressly stated the continued significance of customary law. In the 1907 Hague Convention Number IV, for instance, the "High Contracting Parties" agreed that in cases not covered by specific articles "the inhabitants and belligerants [sic] remain under the protection and the rule of the principles of the law of nations, as they result from the usages established among civilized peoples, from the laws of humanity, and from the dictates of the public conscience."[3] In addition, a common article in each of the 1949 Geneva conventions uses similar terminology in reaffirming customary international law.[4]

The core principles of the nebulous body of customary international law have been identified as military necessity, avoidance of unnecessary suffering, and proportionality.[5] These principles apply to all nations at war even if individual nations have not acceded to the international agreements.[6] All three principles are always present in international conflicts as a means to analyze questionable tactics for which no specific articles apply.

The concept of military necessity provides that a combatant is justified in applying any force necessary to secure the complete submission of the enemy as soon as possible—as long as the means are not prohibited by provisions of the laws of war.[7] In other words, there must be some legitimate military purpose to an action—each destructive act must be connected to the submission of the enemy.[8] The principle was articulated in writing as early as 1868 in the Declaration of St. Petersburg, which stated that "the only legitimate object which states should endeavor to accomplish during war is to weaken the military forces of the enemy."[9]

Military forces at war must also take all possible measures to avoid inflicting unnecessary suffering. It is a violation of customary international law to needlessly aggravate the suffering of the enemy or of civilian populations. The concept of unnecessary suffering may be said to derive from the venerable principles of chivalry and humanity, which forbid resorting to dishonorable means, expedients, or conduct in the course of armed hostility and any use of force not actually necessary for military purposes.[10] The requirement to avoid unnecessary suffering has been codified in the modern agreements as well, as it is forbidden to "employ arms, projectiles, or material calculated to cause unnecessary suffering."[11]

Finally, the principle of proportionality operates as a sort of balancing test between the concepts of military necessity and unnecessary suffering. Under this principle, loss of life and property damage cannot be out of proportion to the military advantage to be gained.[12] The rule of proportionality may also have descended from the traditional principle of humanity, which prohibits the use of unnecessary force.[13] The idea of balancing military necessity and unnecessary suffering seems to have been on the minds of the drafters of the Declaration of St. Petersburg, as well, when they stated that the principle of the declaration would be violated "by the employment of arms which would needlessly aggravate the sufferings of disabled men, or render their death inevitable."[14] Although the laws of war were originally concerned mainly with the protection of human life, as Dr. Boelaert-Suominen states, "it is now generally accepted that the proportionality rule serves to protect the environment as well."[15]

The principles of military necessity, avoidance of unnecessary suffering, and proportionality can be used to discourage not only conventional suffering caused by war but environmental damage as well. After all, severe environmental damages can cause tremendous suffering among war zone populations. Customary international law, in effect, compels commanders to consider potential environmental ramifications of combat actions and to weigh them against the expected tactical advantage.

The Hague and Geneva Conventions

In addition to the framework established by the customary principles of international law, a series of relatively modern conventions began at The Hague in 1899.[16] These conventions, convened first at The Hague and later in Geneva, codified some of the principles of customary law that were recognized at the time. In addition, they established specific prohibitions against certain actions during armed conflicts.

Of The Hague conventions, it is the 1907 Hague Convention Number IV that provides the articles relevant to environmental protection during wartime.[17] Under Article 22, in the annex to the convention, "The right of belligerents to adopt means of injuring the enemy is not unlimited."[18] That article sets the tone for a series of articles that limit means of injuring the enemy.

Article 23 sets out a series of specific prohibitions.[19] It is "especially forbidden," for instance, to "employ poison or poisoned weapons."[20] The provision that restates the customary rule by forbidding arms "calculated to cause unnecessary suffering" is also set forth in Article 23.[21]

Under Article 23 it is also forbidden "to destroy or seize the enemy's property, unless such destruction or seizure be imperatively demanded by the necessities of war."[22] U.S. Marine Corps Major Walter Sharp argued that if the environment is considered part of the enemy's property, this article offers "substantial environmental protection."[23] Antoine Bouvier, of the International Committee of the Red Cross (ICRC), described the provision as "one of the earliest provisions for the protection of environment in armed conflict."[24]

Other provisions of the 1907 Hague Convention Number IV can also be applied for environmental protection under certain circumstances. For instance, the convention forbids confiscation of private property.[25] In addition, "pillage is formally forbidden" by Article 47.[26] Also, when occupying enemy territory, the occupying force is required to administer the "real estate, forests and agricultural estates" of the occupied nation, and "safeguard the capital of these properties, and administer them in accordance with the rules of usufruct."[27] This places a responsibility on occupying forces to care for the natural resources of the occupied territory. This could be considered analogous to the public trust doctrine in U.S. domestic law, which requires the government to administer public property as caretakers for the public.[28]

Each major international conflict seems to spawn a new wave of reform in international law. The use of poisonous gas during World War I, for instance, inspired the 1925 Geneva Gas Protocol.[29] Moreover, the Geneva conventions of 1949, in response to the horrors of the Holocaust, included new protections for civilians against such abuse as torture, medical experiments, and extermination.[30]

Although Nazi crimes of World War II were foremost on the drafters' minds, the Geneva conventions of 1949 also built upon the foundation established at The Hague for environmental protection. Article 53 of Geneva Convention IV, for instance, prohibits "any destruction by the Occupying Power of real or personal property . . . except where such destruction is rendered absolutely necessary by military operations."[31] Thus, wanton destruction of natural resources is prohibited by this convention as well.[32]

Colonel James Terry, of the U.S. Marine Corps, has argued that the primary significance of the 1949 Geneva conventions are the enforcement provisions.[33] Pursuant to common articles in each of the four conventions, signatory nations must identify and address all grave breaches of the conventions.[34] In addition, another article common to each convention requires penal sanctions.[35] This article requires that each nation investigate alleged grave breaches and either try offenders before their own courts or turn them over to the aggrieved nation for trial. Grave breaches are those acts "committed against persons or property" including "willful killing, torture or inhuman treatment, including biological experiments, willfully causing great suffering or serious injury to body or health, and extensive destruction and appropriation of property, not justified by military necessity and carried out unlawfully and wantonly."[36] Colonel Terry argues that when combined with Article 3 of the 1907 Hague Convention IV, which provides for reparations to aggrieved parties, these provisions can provide an effective enforcement tool.[37]

In 1996, the United States adopted the War Crimes Act, which made war crimes a matter of domestic U.S. law and provided for criminal punishments.[38] It specifically includes violations of Article 23 of the 1907 Hague Convention IV and grave breaches of all the 1949 Geneva conventions in its definition of war crimes.[39] War crimes may result in fines consistent with fines established for other federal offenses, imprisonment, "and if death results to the victim, shall be subject to the penalty of death."[40] The statute applies in circumstances in which either the person committing the crime or the victim is a member of the U.S. military or a U.S. national.[41]

The Law of Peace and International Environmental Law

Generally, the conduct of parties in warfare is governed by the laws of war as encompassed by customary laws of war and the Geneva and Hague Conventions—*jus in bello*. However, there is also a general prohibition against unlawful aggression that may also come into play in weighing a nation's culpability for environmental damage in warfare. "By limiting resort to armed force in international relations, *jus ad bellum* aims at reducing the incidence of armed conflict and consequently environmental damage as well," wrote Dr. Boelaert-Suominen.[42] She cited the importance of Article 2(4) of the United Nations Charter in establishing the concept that war must be avoided.[43] "All Members shall refrain in their international relations from the threat or use of force against the territorial integrity or political independence of any state," the charter states, "or in any manner inconsistent with the Purposes of the United Nations."[44] It was on the basis of Iraq's unlawful aggression, in fact, that United Nations Security Council imposed cease-fire conditions on Iraq under Security Council Resolution 687.[45] "Resolution 687 is unique in that environmental damage is expressly and prominently dealt with in the contest of war reparations," wrote Dr. Boelaert-Suominen.[46] There are several drawbacks of using the *jus ad bellum* concept as a basis for addressing infliction of environmental damages in wartime. The primary problem is that it tends to be victor's justice—with the nonaggressor facing no restrictions on its conduct. In addition, it doesn't provide guidance for specific conduct—other than initiating a war—that is prohibited.

In addition, it is unclear to what extent the many international environmental treaties governing peacetime activities would apply during warfare. Dr. Boelaert-Suominen asserted it's generally believed that peacetime international environmental law applies only to the extent that it is consistent with the overarching requirements of national defense and the laws of war.[48] Principle 24 of the Rio Declaration sums up this view when, in recognizing the threat warfare poses to sustainable development, it declares that nations must "respect international law providing protection for the environment in times of armed conflict and co-operate in its further development, as necessary."[49] The kinds of damages inflicted by military activities, however, are often outside the scope of the peacetime environmental treaties, which would also lack the criminal penalties that are encompassed by the laws of war.

The 1977 Geneva Protocols and the ENMOD Convention

Other provisions in international law that limit environmental destruction can be found in Protocol I of the 1977 Protocols Additional to the Geneva Conventions of 1949 and in the 1977 Convention on the Prohibition of Military or Any Other Hostile Use of Environmental Modification Techniques (ENMOD Convention).[50] Neither of these agreements have been universally adopted to this day and neither had been adopted, specifically, by Iraq at the time of the first Persian Gulf War.[51]

Two articles of Protocol I specifically address the protection of the environment in wartime.[52] Article 35 of Protocol I restates the earlier principles that the right to choose means of warfare "is not unlimited" and that it is prohibited to employ "methods of warfare of a nature to cause superfluous injury or unnecessary suffering."[53] But Article 35(3) takes this protection a step further by stating that "it is prohibited to employ methods or means of warfare which are intended, or may be expected, to cause widespread, long-term and severe damage to the natural environment."[54]

Further, Article 55 to the 1977 Geneva Protocol I is concerned entirely with protection of the natural environment.[55] It states the following: "1. Care shall be taken in warfare to protect the natural environment against widespread, long-term and severe damage. This protection includes a prohibition of the use of methods or means of warfare which are intended or may be expected to cause such damage to the natural environment and thereby prejudice the health or survival of the population. 2. Attacks against the natural environment by way of reprisals are prohibited."[56] In addition, Article 56 prohibits attacks on dams, dikes, and "nuclear electrical generating stations" if such attacks would "cause the release of dangerous forces and consequent severe losses among the civilian population."[57]

For those interested in environmental considerations during wartime, Articles 35 and 55 are encouraging because they reflect a growing international trend toward concern for the natural environment, but they have been criticized as being too broad and too vague. Both provisions proscribe methods of combat that would cause "widespread, long-term and severe damage," but neither define "widespread, long-term and severe."[58] "Neither of these articles set forth any workable standards for a commander in the midst of an armed conflict," wrote Major Sharp, adding that "neither articulates a threshold for prohibited environmental destruction."[59] In fact, it could be argued that certain weapons presently in the United States' arsenal—even weapons used in the 1991 and 2003 wars with Iraq—could be construed as causing prohibited environmental damages even when used for intended purposes. Dropping bombs causes environmental damage. Cluster bombs, for instance, are intended to have a devastating effect on target areas. While it was not likely the intent of Articles 35 and 55 to prohibit use of this weapon, the inexactness of the language leaves the articles' intent open to debate—raising the potential that the routine use of cluster bombs during the 1991 Persian Gulf War might have been considered by some to violate the 1977 Protocol I because of the bombs' potentially long-term effects.

Commentators have also criticized other language of the articles. It was argued, for instance, that the "may be expected" language in Article 35(3) "provided a legal ground for challenging the use of any weapon that may affect the environment"—that legitimate weapons could be barred.[60] This arguably leaves open the potential that a commander could be charged with a violation of the 1977 Protocol I if he or she acts against a legitimate military target but causes unintended collateral damage to the environment. Under the language of the 1977 Protocol I, the fact that the damage was not intentional is irrelevant if it could have been "expected." U.S. commanders are trained to aggressively and decisively pursue legitimate military objectives. Holding commanders responsible for unintended environmental consequences would unnecessarily complicate their decisions, potentially undermining the aggressiveness and decisiveness of our commanders.

The United States has never ratified 1977 Geneva Protocol I.[61] In 1987, President Ronald Reagan submitted Protocol II for Senate approval but concluded that Protocol I was "fundamentally and irreconcilably flawed" and declined to submit it to the Senate.[62] The primary reason for rejecting Protocol I, however, was not the environmental provisions but rather that it might have accorded international law protections to terrorist groups.[63] Abraham Sofaer, of the U.S. Department of State, summarized the criticisms of Protocol I by stating that it granted irregular forces a legal status at times "superior to that accorded regular forces; that it unreasonably restricts attacks against certain objects that have traditionally been legitimate targets; and that it eliminates significant remedies in cases where an enemy violates the Protocol."[64] Sofaer, however, did not specifically criticize the environmental articles.[65]

Although neither Iraq nor the United States adopted the 1977 Geneva Protocol I, commentators have speculated that the environmental provisions of Protocol I might be enforceable as customary international law.[66] Customary law is generally limited to those principles that, over time, are adopted through the traditions and practices of nations. Some traditional humanitarian principles of customary international law enunciated in Protocol I, such as the requirement for humane medical attention and respect for medical units, have been adopted and generally followed by all nations.[67] However, the environmental provisions are likely too new, original, and unestablished to constitute traditional norms encompassing customary international law.

The other 1977 conference, ENMOD, was more limited in scope.[68] It was intended to prohibit the military use of climate modification techniques, although some may read it more broadly. In substance, it prohibits the use of environmental modification techniques that are intended to cause, or could be expected to cause, "widespread, long-lasting, or severe" destruction or damage to the enemy.[69] Environmental modification techniques are not clearly defined in the treaty, although they are widely believed to include weather modification.[70] Although many nations have not signed the treaty, the argument has been made that it should be honored as an emerging doctrine of customary international law.[71] Other commentators, however, have concluded that the ENMOD Convention does not constitute customary international law, because its concepts are too new to have been incorporated into nations' conduct of war or their concepts of traditional humanitarian law.[71] Even if Iraq had been a signatory to the ENMOD Convention, wrote John Alan Cohan, Iraqi actions during the 1991 war would not have constituted a violation of that convention because they did not use the environment as a "weapon."[72]

Notes

1. Eric Talbot Jensen, *The International Law of Environmental Warfare: Active and Passive Damage during Armed Conflict*, 38 Vand. J. Transnatl. L. 145, 154 (2005).
2. Adam Roberts and Richard Guelff, Documents on the Laws of War, 2nd ed., 4 (1989).

3. 1907 Hague Convention No. IV, *Respecting the Laws and Customs of War on Land*, Oct. 18, 1907, Preamble, 36 Stat. 2277, 75 U.N.T.S. 287, reprinted in DEPARTMENT OF THE ARMY, PAMPHLET NO. 27-1, TREATIES GOVERNING LAND WARFARE 5 (1956).

4. ROBERTS AND GUELFF, DOCUMENTS, supra note 2, at 4–5.

5. L. Lynn Hogue, *Identifying Customary International Law of War in Protocol I: A Proposed Restatement*, 13 LOY. L.A. INTL. & COMP. L.J. 279, 297 (1990).

6. DEPARTMENT OF THE ARMY, FIELD MANUAL 27-10, THE LAW OF LAND WARFARE 6 (1956).

7. ROBERTS AND GUELFF, DOCUMENTS, supra note 2, at 5–6.

8. Walter G. Sharp, *The Effective Deterrence of Environmental Damage during Armed Conflict: A Case Analysis of the Persian Gulf War*, 137 MIL. L. REV. 1, 30 (1992).

9. DEPARTMENT OF THE ARMY, PAMPHLET NO. 27-161-2, INTERNATIONAL LAW, VOLUME II 40 (1962).

10. ROBERTS AND GUELFF, DOCUMENTS, supra note 2, at 5.

11. 1907 Hague Convention No. IV, *Respecting the Laws*, art. 23(e), 36 Stat., at 2302.

12. DEPARTMENT OF THE ARMY, THE LAW OF LAND WARFARE, supra note 6, at 19. See also Guy B. Roberts, *The New Rules for Waging War: The Case Against Ratification of Additional Protocol I*, 26 VA. J. OF INTL. L. 109, 117–18 (1985).

13. ROBERTS AND GUELFF, DOCUMENTS, supra note 2, at 5.

14. DEPARTMENT OF THE ARMY, INTERNATIONAL LAW, supra note 9, at 40.

15. SONJA ANN JOZEF BOELAERT-SUOMINEN, INTERNATIONAL ENVIRONMENTAL LAW AND NAVAL WAR 4 (2000) (Newport Paper Number Fifteen, Center for Naval Warfare Studies, Naval War College).

16. Sharp, *The Effective Deterrence*, supra note 8, at 7. See also James P. Terry, *The Environment and the Laws of War: The Impact of Desert Storm*, 45 NAVAL WAR C. REV. 61, 62 (1992).

17. Terry, *The Environment and the Laws of War*, supra note 16, at 62. Interestingly, Iraq never formally adopted the 1907 Hague Convention No. IV. At that time Iraq had been part of the Ottoman Empire, which did not become a party to the convention. Afterward, Iraq became a British Protectorate, but Britain apparently never acceded to the convention on behalf of Iraq. However, Iraq is bound by customary law encoded in the convention (Sharp, *The Effective Deterrence*, supra note 8, at 8–9).

18. 1907 Hague Convention No. IV, *Respecting the Laws*, art. 22, 36 Stat., at 2301.

19. *Id.* art. 23, 36 Stat., at 2301.

20. *Id.* art. 23(a), 36 Stat., at 2301.

21. *Id.* art. 23(e), 36 Stat., at 2301.

22. *Id.* art. 23(g), 36 Stat., at 2301.

23. Sharp, *The Effective Deterrence*, supra note 8, at 11.

24. Antoine Bouvier, *Protection of the Natural Environment in Time of Armed Conflict*, 285 INTL. REV. RED CROSS 567, 572 (1991).

25. 1907 Hague Convention No. IV, *Respecting the Laws*, art. 46, 36 Stat., at 2306.

26. *Id.* art. 47, 36 Stat., at 2307.

27. *Id.* art. 55, 36 Stat., at 2307.

28. See, e.g., Illinois Central Railroad v. Illinois, 146 U.S. 387 (1892).

29. 1925 Geneva Protocol for the Prohibition of the Use in War of Asphyxiating, Poisonous, or Other Gases and of Bacteriological Methods of Warfare, June 17, 1925, 26 U.S.T. 571, T.A.I.S. No. 8061, reprinted in ROBERTS AND GUELFF, DOCUMENTS, supra note 2, at 37–145.

30. 1949 Geneva Convention No. IV, art. 32, 6 U.S.T. at 3538, 75 U.N.T.S. at 310.

31. *Id.* art. 53, 6 U.S.T. at 3552, 75 U.N.T.S. at 322.

32. Terry, *The Environment and the Laws of War*, supra note 16, at 63.

33. *Id.*

34. See 1949 Geneva Convention No. I, art. 51, 6 U.S.T. at 3148, 75 U.N.T.S. at 64; 1949 Geneva Convention No. III, art. 131, 6 U.S.T. at 3420, 75 U.N.T.S. at 238; 1949 Geneva Convention No. IV, 6 U.S.T. at 3518, 75 U.N.T.S. at 388.

35. See 1949 Geneva Convention No. I, art. 49, 6 U.S.T. at 3146, 75 U.N.T.S. at 62; 1949 Geneva Convention No. II, art. 50, 6 U.S.T. at 3250, 75 U.N.T.S. at 116; 1949 Geneva Convention No. III, art. 129, 6 U.S.T. at 3418, 75 U.N.T.S. at 236; 1949 Geneva Convention No. IV, art. 146, 6 U.S.T. at 3616, 75 U.N.T.S. at 386.

36. See 1949 Geneva Convention No. I, art 50, 6 U.S.T. at 3147, 75 U.N.T.S. at 63; 1949 Geneva Convention No. II, art. 51, 6 U.S.T. at 3251, 75 U.N.T.S. at 117; 1949 Geneva Convention No. III, art. 130, 6 U.S.T. at 3419, 75 U.N.T.S. at 237; 1949 Geneva Convention No. IV, art. 147, 6 U.S.T. at 3617, 75 U.N.T.S. at 387.

37. Terry, *The Environment and the Laws of War*, supra note 16, at 63.

38. 18 U.S.C. § 2441.

39. *Id.* § 2441(c).

40. *Id.* § 2441(a).

41. *Id.* § 2441(b).

42. BOELAERT-SUOMINEN, INTERNATIONAL ENVIRONMENTAL LAW, supra note 15, at 73.

43. *Id.* at 71.

44. UN Charter art. 2, para. 4.

45. UN SCOR 687, Apr. 3, 1991.

46. BOELAERT-SUOMINEN, INTERNATIONAL ENVIRONMENTAL LAW, supra note 15, at 76.

47. *Id.* at 73.

48. CONVENTION ON BIOLOGICAL DIVERSITY, Rio de Janeiro, 31 ILM 822 (June 5, 1992).

49. Terry, *The Environment and the Laws of War*, supra note 16, at 64–65.

50. *Id.*

51. 1977 Protocol Additional to the Geneva Conventions of 12 August 1949, and Relating to the Protection of Victims of International Armed Conflicts, Dec. 12, 1977, 1125 U.N.T.S. 3, reprinted in DEPARTMENT OF THE ARMY, PAMPHLET 27-1-1 (1979).

52. 1977 Protocol Additional, arts. 35(1) and (2), 1125 U.N.T.S. at 21.

53. *Id.* art. 35(3), 1125 U.N.T.S., at 21.

54. *Id.* art. 55, 1125 U.N.T.S., at 28.

55. *Id.*

56. *Id.* art. 56, 1125 U.N.T.S., at 28.

57. See *id.* art. 35(3), 1125 U.N.T.S., at 21; *Id.* art. 55(1), 1125 U.N.T.S., at 32.

58. Sharp, *The Effective Deterrence*, supra note 8, at 16.

59. Roberts, *The New Rules*, supra note 12, at 147.

60. Terry, *The Environment and the Laws of War*, supra note 16, at 64.

61. Ronald Reagan, *Agora: The Decision Not to Ratify Protocol I to the Geneva Conventions on the Protection of War Victims: Letter of Transmittal*, 81 AM. J. INTL. L. 910 (1987).

62. *Id.* at 911. See also Abraham D. Sofaer, *Agora: The U.S. Decision Not to Ratify Protocol I to the Geneva Conventions on the Protection of War Victims: The Rationale for the United States Decision*, 82 AM. J. INTL. L. 784 (1988).

63. Sofaer, *Agora*, supra note 62, at 785.

64. *Id.*

65. Sharp, *The Effective Deterrence*, supra note 8, at 14.

66. Hogue, *Identifying Customary International Law*, supra note 5, at 297–302.

67. Terry, *The Environment and the Laws of War*, supra note 16, at 64.

68. ENMOD Convention (Convention on the Prohibition of Military or Any Other Hostile Use of Environmental Modification Techniques), May 18, 1977, 31 U.S.T. 333, 1108 U.N.T.S. 151.

69. WILLIAM M. ARKIN, DAMIAN DURRANT, AND MARIANNE CHERNI, ON IMPACT: MODERN WARFARE AND THE ENVIRONMENT—A XASE STUDY OF THE GULF WAR, 139–40 (1991).

70. *Id.* at 140.

71. See, e.g., Sharp, *The Effective Deterrence*, supra note 8, at 19.

72. John Alan Cohan, *Modes of Warfare and Evolving Standards of Environmental Protection under the International Law of War*, 15 FLA. INTL. L. 481, 524 (2003).

12

Punishing Environmental War Crimes

"ENVIRONMENTAL DAMAGE IN WARTIME IS INEVITABLE," wrote Antoine Bouvier. "Throughout history, war has always left its mark, sometimes extremely long-lasting, on the natural environment."[1] The 1991 Persian Gulf War was no exception. The effect on the fragile desert ecology of thousands of troops and military vehicles cannot be calculated. Yet, it was not merely marching armies and rolling vehicles that caused the tremendous environmental damage to the Gulf region. "The Iraqi occupation of Kuwait," wrote Greenpeace analysts, "and the war to dislodge Iraq, left behind an environmental disaster in the air, in the water, and on the land."[2]

Even the coalition forces, Greenpeace analysts pointed out, caused damages to the environment during the 1991 Gulf War. "For all the efficiency and economy of purpose displayed by allied forces," a Greenpeace report concluded, "the Gulf War was unprecedented in the amount of destruction inflicted on a nation with 'conventional' weapons in so short a period of time. It left a civil society reeling and completely disrupted, and the natural environment unusually scarred."[3] Yet, the Greenpeace report continued, coalition forces for the most part fought within the law. "The U.S. military, and, by example its allies, were constantly mindful of international public opinion. The fear of losing public support influenced military policy from the beginning," Greenpeace analysts wrote. "The war was to be short, with allied casualties to be kept to a minimum. There would be no indiscriminate bombing of civilian targets or cities."[4]

It is part of the purpose of the laws of war to place limits on environmental damage—to prohibit wanton environmental destruction with no legitimate military purpose. So long as a commander has a legitimate military objective, and legitimate military means are employed to achieve that objective, the commander should be able to act with impunity. The United States encourages its commanders at every level to act decisively and aggressively so long as they're within the parameters of legitimate warfare. While war itself, fought by legitimate means, may be tremendously damaging to the environment, it is only war by illegitimate means that is prohibited by existing principles of international law.

The Iraqi leadership after the 1991 war doubtless could have been accused of multiple war crimes for its acts during the Persian Gulf War. Its treatment of prisoners and Kuwaiti civilians during occupation led to many violations as did its unprovoked launching of missiles at Israel, a noncombatant nation. Yet, what seems to have set Saddam Hussein apart from history's other despots was the seemingly spiteful environmental terrorism carried out by his troops, especially the intentional releases of oil into the Persian Gulf and the multiple oil well fires set in Kuwait. "These acts are clearly gross violations of all the specific and implied environmental property protections which exist in the laws of war," the Greenpeace study concluded.[5]

The general principles of international law encompassed by customary law and the Geneva and Hague conventions do provide sufficient grounds for punishing intentional Iraqi environmental damage in the 1991 Persian Gulf War, had any of the coalition allies sought such punishment. It would have been unnecessary to consider whether the sanctions of the 1977 Geneva Protocol I or the ENMOD Convention (Convention on the Prohibition of Military or Any Other Hostile Use of Environmental Modification Techniques) applied to Iraq, since the same environmental terrorism that might give rise to charges under those agreements could be charged under international laws that clearly applied to Iraq. In fact, in the case of Protocol I, it would not have been sound policy to argue that its vague prohibitions should apply to Iraq when the United States itself was not comfortable with its language.

Under customary law, Iraq might have been able to articulate tenuous military purposes for dumping the oil and igniting the Kuwaiti wells—to hinder a sea landing in the case of the oil spills and to provide cover from air attack in the case of the oil fires. However, the weak argument that Iraq took the actions out of military necessity would have been overcome by the principle of proportionality. The minor military purposes were not reasonably worth the environmental damages caused. This is particularly true with respect to destruction of Kuwait's oil wells, since evidence would be likely to indicate Iraq carefully planned. "Iraq actually did experiments to see how to best blow up a wellhead, and started wiring the wells soon after the invasion [in August 1990]," Greenpeace analysts wrote.[6]

The Iraqi leadership also violated several specific prohibitions set forth in the Hague and Geneva Conventions. Both the oil spill and the destruction of the oil wells could be considered prohibited destruction of the enemy's property under Article 23 of the 1907 Hague Convention Number IV.[7] In addition, these acts could be considered prohibited "pillage" as well as violations of an occupying state's responsibility to safeguard property in the occupied territory.[8] Geneva Convention IV of 1949 also prohibits destruction of real or personal property absent military necessity.[9]

However, whatever violations Iraqi leaders may have committed during the 1991 Persian Gulf War went uncharged. Under the 1949 Geneva conventions every signatory nation has the responsibility to identify and address, and then to sanction, offenders.[10] Since any participant in a conflict would have jurisdiction to subject an individual to adjudication under the international laws of armed conflict, the Iraqi leadership could have been brought before a tribunal after the 1991 conflict. Yet, probably because of sensitive political concerns, no nation ever took the lead in bringing the Iraqi leadership to justice until 2003, in a conflict entered under premises based mainly on issues other than the behavior of Iraqi forces during the 1991 conflict.

The Call for New Law

As a result of the tremendous environmental devastation during the 1991 Persian Gulf War, there came in the 1990s a heightened interest in the world community in the sufficiency of international law to protect the environment in combat. International law already in effect provided sufficient means to discourage needless environmental destruction during wartime if the law is enforced. Critics of existing law, however, referred derisively to the environmental protections in the laws of war as "indirect."[11] They argued that the laws of war did not sufficiently discourage environmental destruction.[12]

Greenpeace analysts argued, for instance, that the laws of war were fundamentally flawed. The Greenpeace writers also argued that since commanders in proper circumstances could subordinate environmental concerns to military necessity, there was little restriction on damage.[13] While Greenpeace did not specifically recommend any action in its 1991 report on the Persian Gulf War, its conclusion appeared to be that the international community should opt to specifically prohibit more war fighting practices.[14]

Greenpeace and others have also urged the formal adoption of the 1977 Geneva Protocol I as a means for providing enhanced protection of the environment during wartime, despite its vagueness.[15] The Greenpeace report, for instance, described the 1977 protocols as "the most important instruments relating to the conduct of warfare and the natural environment."[16] Judge George Aldrich has argued that concerns with the vagueness of the language are unfounded and that the environmental articles would not limit conventional warfare.[17] He opined, for instance that "long-term" should be "understood in terms of decades."[18]

However, the fact remains that the environmental articles of the 1977 Geneva Protocol I are vaguely worded, despite Judge Aldrich's declaration. New environmental protections in international law may be inevitable, but the United States must ensure that it can comply with even the most farfetched interpretations of their language. If terms such as "long-term" or "widespread" are used to describe prohibited environmental damage, then those terms must be defined in the instruments themselves rather than risking the possibility that one of our captured war fighters could be placed on trial for "violations" by an enemy under some tortured interpretation of the language. Staging such a "war crimes" trial against one of our young fighters could be an effective propaganda weapon for an enemy.

In addition, the United States' ability to respond militarily to a threat should not be compromised. As Colonel James Terry explained, "Only through a military capability such as reflected in the coalition reaction to Iraqi aggression can the environment, in the long term, best be preserved."[19] In other words, international law should not constrict "the prudent use of modern weapon systems" to respond to violent aggression.[20] The United States and its coalition allies in 1991 were able to suppress aggression in the Gulf with astoundingly low casualties. Had commanders been prohibited from using certain weapon systems, the war may have been more costly in allied lives.

Further, laws of war that are too restrictive of legitimate use of force may tend to penalize nations that follow the law. Nations that follow the law will likely come to depend on enemy nations' compliance. For instance, weapon systems that are perceived as illegal may be discarded as obsolete, leaving no means to respond to the hostile use of similar weapons. Historically, nations have violated accepted international treaties when they saw a distinct military advantage for themselves. During World War II, for instance, Germany routinely violated the London Convention on Submarine Warfare of 1936 by sinking surface vessels without giving advance warning.[21] Since the allies had relied on Germany's compliance with the convention and developed no ready means for combating this strategy, Germany's strategy was effective.[22]

The concerns of international environmentalists that the environment is not prominently considered in the laws of war are understandable. While protections for the environment do exist in the laws of war, a tribunal would likely be required to "back door" the environmental charges by charging other crimes. Still, the United States must take caution not to adopt an unacceptable environmental article. Any language ultimately incorporated into binding international law must be protective of legitimate weapon systems and sufficiently well defined to prevent severe misinterpretations by enemy nations. If the United States was to formally adopt language similar to that set forth in the Geneva Protocol I, the final language should not be speculative or vague, as is the present language. For example, the articles might arguably be more acceptable if the "or may be expected" language was eliminated from Articles 35(3) and 55. Thus, actions such as Iraq's environmental terrorism would be explicitly barred since their primary intent was to cause environmental damage, but legitimate conventional warfare with unintended environmental damages would not. In addition, the terms "widespread, long-term, and severe" should each be separately defined.

Another approach that has been proposed is to strengthen the enforceability of the laws of armed conflict so that sanctions present a real deterrent to environmental terrorism or the intentional infliction of environmental damage as a military tactic. This approach is driven by the assumption that some nations will not comply with a law they do not respect and that those nations will not respect a law unless there is a reasonable expectation that someone will attempt to enforce it. U.S. military service members worldwide are subject to the Uniform Code of Military Justice, which provides a means to prosecute violations of the law of war.[23] With respect to other nations, however, it has been argued that only an international tribunal would provide sufficient assurance that environmental war crimes would be prosecuted. Major Walter Sharp called in 1992 for the adoption of a permanent international court with independence to operate apart from the influence of any one nation.[24] With such a court, he argued, nations could not interfere with prosecutions because of political concerns.[25] This approach would make war crimes prosecutions more frequent, but such a court would still be forced to rely on the initiative of nations to enforce its decisions.

However, the President George W. Bush administration, fearing that such a court might use its jurisdiction to conduct politically motivated investigations and prosecutions of U.S. citizens, on May 6, 2002, withdrew U.S. support from the treaty creating the International Criminal Court (ICC), which had been previously signed by President William Clinton in 2000.[26] "I think [withdrawal from the treaty] is a very backwards step," said Yugoslavia war crimes tribunal judge Richard Goldstone. "It is unprecedented which I think to an extent smacks of pettiness in the sense that it is not going to affect in any way the establishment of the International Criminal Court. The U.S. have really isolated themselves and are putting themselves into bed with the likes of China, the Yemen and other undemocratic countries."[27] Secretary of State Colin Powell, however, said that the Bush administration was concerned with the court's lack of accountability to U.S. judicial authority or even to the United Nations Security Council.[28]

The Bush administration cited legitimate concerns and reflected the skepticism about joint international action held by a segment of the U.S. population. By rejecting the International Criminal Court outright, however, the Bush administration foreclosed the remedy many have recommended to ensure that war criminals, including those committing environmental war crimes, are brought to justice. Rejecting the court, if the United States' lead had been universally followed, would have reestablished the tradition of independent, sporadic enforcement that has been the norm in the past. A number of nations, including Spain, Australia, Uruguay, and others, entered the ICC agreement, the Rome Statute of the International Criminal Court,[29] with written declarations.[30] Under Article 120 of the Rome Statute, nations cannot make reservations to the treaty, a procedure traditionally employed to note provisions within the treaty or circumstances under which a signatory nation would not comply.[31] But, with respect to the Rome Statute, several signatory nations composed "declarations" that elaborated those nations' understandings of the statute. In some cases, those declarations were so explicit as to almost amount to reservations. Spain, for instance, declared it would be willing to imprison an individual convicted by the court but only if "the duration of the sentence does not exceed the maximum stipulated for any crime under Spanish law."[32] Similarly, Australia declared its belief that the ICC would not act in cases that are being actively investigated or prosecuted by an individual signatory; reaffirmed "the primacy of its criminal jurisdiction in relation to crimes within the jurisdiction of the Court"; and declared its "understanding" that several provisions "will be interpreted and applied in a way that accords with the way they are implemented in Australian domestic law."[33] Uruguay subtly made the statute subject to its own law by declaring that it acceded to the statute "insofar as it is competent in that respect and in strict accordance with the constitutional provisions of the Republic." Rather than rejecting the statute outright, the United States could have explored a means to ratify the agreement with its concerns reflected in a written declaration. The United States as a sovereign would also have had the option to withdraw from the agreement if the court were to operate in a manner inconsistent with U.S. law or the rights of its citizens. The court went into operation in 2002, however, without the participation of the United States.[34]

The Course for the Future

Traditionally, in the wake of every major war there is some international concern to correct the great injustices of the preceding war. After World War I, the burning concern was to limit chemical weapons. After World War II, the concern was to prevent the repetition of the Holocaust. Since the 1991 Persian Gulf War, the international community has been more concerned with strengthening environmental protection in wartime. However, existing principles of international law already prohibit most of the actions that caused the terrible environmental damage during the first war with Iraq. Under that existing law Saddam Hussein and the responsible Iraqi leadership could have been held accountable for the environmental devastation in the 1991 Persian Gulf War. An expansion of law would have been unnecessary. Still, some compromise provisions may be eventually inevitable to address the concern over environmental destruction. The United States should not be afraid to engage in a dialogue aimed toward getting specific environmental provisions into formal articles in the conventions. It is a means to emphasize the growing importance of the environment in all legal regimes. Such specific environmental protections for war could be acceptable to the United States if properly drafted so that they do not hinder the national defense and if sufficient means exist to ensure compliance. As yet, there has been no major international move to tighten up the language of environmental provisions within the laws of war, but the concern over the adequacy of environmental protections in the international laws of war persists. In 2003, for instance, United Nations Secretary General Kofi Annan called for tougher laws to protect the environment during warfare. "Ensuring environmental sustainability is not a luxury; it is a prerequisite for the future peace and prosperity of our planet," he said.[35] He also said that while there have been relatively few instances in which the environment was deliberately target, gray areas remained in which more care should be taken to protect the environment during military operations. In support of Annan's comments, Executive Director Klaus Toepfer, of the UN Environment Program, asked rhetorically, "Should striking an oil tanker sailing near a coral reef be deemed unacceptable, or a legitimate act of war? Does the crippling of an enemy's oil supplies justify the killing of an ecosystem upon which hundreds, maybe thousands, of the poor rely for food in the form of fish?"[36]

The establishment of the International Criminal Court was a major step toward ensuring compliance, but the United States' subsequent rejection of the court negated much of the momentum that had been generated toward international accountability for environmental terrorism during warfare. The decision to withdraw U.S. support from the court, while based upon legitimate concerns, should be revisited. An option might be to ratify the agreement with a written reservation. The United States should find a way to participate, along with the rest of the world community, in this endeavor.

Notes

1. Antoine Bouvier, *Protection of the Natural Environment in Time of Armed Conflict*, 285 INTL. REV. RED CROSS 567, 569 (1991).
2. WILLIAM M. ARKIN, DAMIAN DURRANT, AND MARIANNE CHERNI, ON IMPACT: MODERN WARFARE AND THE ENVIRONMENT—A CASE STUDY OF THE GULF WAR 16 (1991).
3. *Id.* at 5.
4. *Id.* at 7.
5. *Id.* at 21.
6. *Id.* at 66.
7. 1907 Hague Convention No. IV, art. 23, 36 Stat., at 2301.
8. See *id.* art. 47, 36 Stat., at 2301; *id.* art. 55, 36 Stat., at 2309.
9. 1949 Geneva Convention No. IV, art. 53, 6 U.S.T. at 3552, 75 U.N.T.S. at 322.
10. See *id.* art. 146, 6 U.S.T. at 3616, 75 U.N.T.S. at 386.
11. Bouvier, *Protection of the Natural Environment*, supra note 1, at 571. But, see Michael D. Diederich, *"Law of War" and Ecology—A Proposal for a Workable Approach to Protecting the Environment through the Law of War*, 136 MIL. L. REV. 137 (1992).
12. ARKIN, DURRANT, AND CHERNI, ON IMPACT, supra note 2, at 22.
13. *Id.* at 114–24. For a counterpoint to Greenpeace's argument, see, e.g., William A. Wilcox Jr., *Environmental Protection in Combat*, 17 S. ILL. U. L.J. 299 (1993).
14. ARKIN, DURRANT, AND CHERNI, ON IMPACT, supra note 2, at 114–24.
15. *Id.* at 123; Bouvier, *Protection of the Natural Environment*, supra note 1, at 577; George H. Aldrich, *Progressive Development of the Laws of War: A Reply to the Criticisms of the 1977 Geneva Protocol I*, 26 VA. J. INTL. L. 693, 711 (1986).
16. ARKIN, DURRANT, AND CHERNI, ON IMPACT, supra note 2, at 123.
17. Aldrich, *Progressive Development*, supra note 15, at 711.
18. *Id.*
19. James P. Terry, *The Environment and the Laws of War: The Impact of Desert Storm*, 45 NAVAL WAR C. REV. 61 (1992).
20. *Id.* at 66.
21. DAVID ZIEGLER, WAR, PEACE, AND INTERNATIONAL POLITICS 154–55 (1977).
22. *Id.*
23. 10 U.S.C. § 801 et seq. See Eric Talbot Jensen and James J. Teixeira Jr., *Prosecuting Members of the U.S. Military for Wartime Environmental Crimes*, 17 GEO. INTL. ENVTL. L. REV. 651 (2005).
24. Walter G. Sharp, *The Effective Deterrence of Environmental Damage during Armed Conflict: A Case Analysis of the Persian Gulf War*, 137 MIL. L. REV. 1, 60–62 (1992).
25. *Id.*

26. BBC, *US Renounces World Court Treaty*, May 6, 2002, http://news.bbc.co.uk/1/hi/world/americas/1970312.stm (accessed Oct. 4, 2005).

27. *Id.*

28. *Id.*

29. *Rome Statute of the International Criminal Court*, July 17, 1998, International Committee for the Red Cross website, www.icrc.org/IHL.nsf/WebPrint/585-FULL?OpenDocument (accessed Oct. 14, 2005).

30. State Parties/Signatories, *Rome Statute of the International Criminal Court*, International Committee for the Red Cross website, www.icrc.org/IHL.nsf/WebSign?ReadForm&id=585&ps=P (accessed Oct. 14, 2005).

31. *Rome Statute*, supra note 30, art. 120.

32. State Parties, *Rome Statute*, supra note 30.

33. *Id.*

34. The Bush administration reportedly has also sought changes in the War Crimes Act, which criminalized violations of the Geneva conventions and certain Hague Convention provisions. See R. Jeffrey Smith, *War Crimes Act Changes Would Reduce Threat of Prosecution*, WASHINGTON POST, Aug. 9, 2006, at 1. The effort to change the law was begun following the Supreme Court's decision in *Hamdan v. Rumsfeld*, 126 S.Ct. 2749 (2006), which overturned the administration's position that the Geneva conventions shouldn't apply to prisoners taken in the United States' 2001 invasion of Afghanistan. The administration has cited vagueness of certain international agreement provisions that trigger the War Crimes Act and has concerns over the way the Act presently operates in seeking changes yet to be introduced in Congress. Common Article 3 of the Geneva conventions, for instance, prohibits "outrages upon personal dignity, in particular, humiliating and degrading treatment"—terms that are not further defined. The Bush administration's proposed changes reportedly would narrow potential criminal prosecutions to ten specific categories, including torture, murder, rape, and hostage taking. The more vague prohibitions of Common Article 3 reportedly would be omitted under the new formulations in the amendment (*Id.*).

35. UN News Service, *Annan Calls for Expanded Laws against Environmental Damage in War*, Nov. 6, 2003, www.un.org/apps/news/printnewsAr.asp?nid=8800 (accessed Oct. 14, 2005).

36. *Id.*

Conclusion: National Security versus Natural Security

BALANCING MILITARY PREPAREDNESS with environmental protection is a mission not easily accomplished. National defense by its very nature involves endangerment to human life. But one principle can be applied both in times of international conflict and in domestic policy making: the military must avoid causing unnecessary suffering. Few would disagree with that premise. But it is in determining what suffering is unnecessary that disagreements can arise. One individual might view an assault on an enemy's power plant for a marginal tactical advantage as unnecessary if it would interrupt the electrical supply to the civilian population's water treatment systems, while another individual might view that same power grid as a vital important tactical target. Differences could occur as to whether the action itself is unnecessary or, if there is a military necessity, as to the means of accomplishing the mission sufficiently without unnecessary suffering. At home, some might view an interruption in training at an installation because of the protection of an endangered species as unacceptable; others might argue that the training should be conducted in less environmentally sensitive locations even if cost of training elsewhere to the military service and to the community surrounding that installation is substantial. One's position on the debate is based largely on individual values and priorities. But a balance between military and environmental needs is achievable in most instances. Certain values are common to almost all of us. Few would disagree that the United States must be prepared to defend itself, and few would disagree that environmental protection is important as well. Sometimes the values are incompatible. Determining which value takes precedence is a challenge, but solutions can often be reached that accommodate both national security interests and natural security interests.

Peacetime Operations

The military preparedness mission at home poses many problems. Defense-related activities comprise a significant part of the United States' environmental challenge. Cleaning up deposits of hazardous materials pollution from past national defense activities at places such as the Department of Energy's Rocky Flats, Colorado, and the Army's Aberdeen Proving Ground, Maryland, is a significant national problem. Regulating present-day military activities amidst heightened environmental concerns and increased worry about domestic security is a perplexing puzzle. Environmental regulators and public interest groups are often frustrated and mystified at what they perceive as preferential treatment of federal government entities because of legal doctrines such as sovereign immunity. For the most part, the modern U.S. military is required to comply with environmental laws in the United States. Federal facilities provisions in each of the major environmental statutes waive sovereign immunity for compliance and, in most statutes, for enforcement. Every branch of the military compels environmental compliance in service regulations.[1] In some respects, such as environmental assessment of proposed federal actions under the National Environmental Policy Act (NEPA),[2] federal agencies including military services are held to higher standards than private sector companies. In other instances, federal agencies do enjoy certain environmental loopholes not available to the private sector—such as relief from payment of civil penalties under certain environmental statutes.[3]

The military services, meanwhile, argue that certain environmental laws impede their ability to train their forces for combat. In recent years Congress has approved a handful of measures that grant some relief in environmental laws to the military services in accomplishment of those training missions. Given the national security exemptions to numerous environmental statutes that already exist, however, Congress should look long and hard before establishing any further exemptions to existing environmental laws for military activities. If relief from environmental requirements is truly required for some military activities, the mechanism is already in place in most environmental laws to grant the relief. The fact that those exemptions are procedurally cumbersome is not a compelling argument for a more sweeping change. Environmental protection is important enough that exemptions from environmental law *should* be cumbersome and should place a high burden on the military to show the need for an exemption. Military planners should explore all potentially less environmentally harmful alternatives to a course of action before seeking an exemption from environmental law.

Access to Environmental Information

Finally, for state and federal regulators, state attorneys general, and the public to effectively hold the military services to their environmental law obligations, information about domestic military operations must be available to the public. The free flow of information is key in providing a basis with which to assess environmental impacts and compliance. By operation of the environmental laws themselves, much of this information is already available. Public notice requirements in obtaining permits, for instance, serve to shine a bright light on potential contributors of pollution on military installations. In addition, the NEPA environmental planning process also requires public involvement.

But the backbone of public information law in the United States is the Freedom of Information Act (FOIA).[4] When enacted in 1964, the FOIA amplified a long-standing tradition of general government openness. The FOIA is a primary tool for the public to obtain environmental information on federal government activities, including military activities. The FOIA should be interpreted and applied as broadly as possible to encourage the sharing of information. The FOIA should not be used as a shield for federal agencies to keep information unnecessarily secret. Yet, the FOIA policy adopted by the Justice Department shortly after the tragedy of September 11, 2001, did just that. It reversed the previous administration's presumption in favor of release with a presumption against release. This decision, based on national security concerns, could have a negative effect on the public's ability to obtain information regarding the environmental performance of domestic military installations.

The Future of Warfare

International conflicts during the past two decades have highlighted the damage that warfare can have on the natural environment. Iraqi efforts to pollute the seas and skies during the Persian Gulf War in 1991 shocked the world, but they were only part of the problem. Warfare by legitimate means also takes its toll. The nature of war is harmful to nature. Combatants typically are locked in a death struggle with an enemy and are primarily concerned with winning. Concerns about collateral damages, whether to people or to the environment, may become subordinate to the military mission (although if a military effort is expected to involve a nation-building effort minimizing collateral damages may still be key in winning the "hearts and minds" of noncombatants). No national leaders are apt to risk sacrificing their citizens' lives by exerting less than their nations' necessary military potential in a conflict. But international law does call for consideration both of potential civilian casualties and of potential damages to the environment. It also makes wanton, unnecessary destruction of the environment illegal. Under existing international law, damages such as those rendered by Iraqi forces in the oil fields of Kuwait and the Persian Gulf could be addressed in war crimes tribunals. The fact that they were not was more attributable to the geopolitical situation than to established international law.

Yet the world community has taken steps to establish a forum to address war crimes in future international military conflicts in a more consistent fashion. The International Criminal Court would provide a means to address environmental war crimes. The United States, however, withdrew its support from that effort. Its decision to reject the international court, which reflected a long-standing mistrust of international institutions by a faction within the United States, should be revisited. Although the United States cited legitimate concerns with regard to the accountability of the court and lack of potential appeals in the event of abuses by the court, the manner in which the United States' foreign policy officials rejected the court foreclosed any discussion about how the officials' concerns might be addressed in the international context.

The Future of the Military and the Environment

Despite the recent weighting of national priorities in favor of defense over the environment, the military has generally improved its environmental compliance over the years. What in the 1980s seemed impossible is now, for the most part, a reality—military installations must comply with the majority of environmental laws. Military leaders now consider environmental management part of the core mission in installation management. But there are still conflicts between the competing values of national defense and natural defense that remain unresolved. With careful consideration of both national defense requirements and environmental needs, acceptable means to accommodate the competing values can normally be found that do not restrict national defense capabilities or unnecessarily harm the environment.

Notes

1. See, e.g., Department of the Army, Reg. 200-1 (1997).
2. 42 U.S.C. § 4321 et seq.
3. See Department of Energy v. Ohio, 503 U.S. 607 (1992).
4. 5 U.S.C. § 552.

Index

About the Author

William A. Wilcox, Jr., practices in the area of environmental law for the Washington, D.C., office of Pillsbury Winthrop Shaw Pittman LLP. He has fifteen years of government environmental, administrative, and procurement law experience. Immediately prior to joining the firm, Mr. Wilcox was the senior environmental attorney for the U.S. Army's Base Realignments and Closures (BRAC) program.

As an active duty officer in the U.S. Army Judge Advocate General's Corps from 1990 until 1995, he served at Aberdeen Proving Ground, Maryland, and Fort Bliss, Texas. He was environmental attorney at Fort Bliss from 1995 until 1998. From 1998 through 2001, Mr. Wilcox served as general counsel for the U.S. Section, International Boundary and Water Commission, United States and Mexico.

A lieutenant colonel in the U.S. Army Reserve, he served on active duty in 2001–2002 following the tragedy of September 11, 2001. Mr. Wilcox is currently a member of the 1st Legal Support Organization, Fort Sam Houston, Texas. He also serves on the editorial board of the *Eastern Water Law and Policy Reporter.* His articles have appeared in such journals as the *Harvard Journal of Law and Public Policy*, the *Villanova Environmental Law Journal*, and the *Land and Water Law Review.*

Milton Keynes UK
Ingram Content Group UK Ltd.
UKHW040801300924
448953UK00026B/149

9 780865 871748